D0854837

PROPERTY OF
LOUISVILLE PUBLIC LIBRARY

GERTRUDE
STEIN

GERTRUDE STEIN

ANN LA FARGE

CHELSEA HOUSE PUBLISHERS

NEW YORK • NEW HAVEN • PHILADELPHIA

J
B
S 34L

Cover: *Gertrude Stein* by Pablo Picasso, 1906

Editor-in-Chief: Nancy Toff
Executive Editor: Remmel T. Nunn
Managing Editor: Karyn Gullen Browne
Copy Chief: Juliann Barbato
Picture Editor: Adrian G. Allen
Art Director: Giannella Garrett
Manufacturing Manager: Gerald Levine

Staff for GERTRUDE STEIN:

Senior Editor: Constance Jones
Text Editor: Marian W. Taylor
Copyeditor: Ellen Scordato
Editorial Assistant: Theodore Keyes
Picture Researcher: Johanna Cypis
Designer: Design Oasis
Production Coordinator: Joseph Romano
Cover Design: Alan J. Nahigian

Creative Director: Harold Steinberg

Copyright © 1988 by Chelsea House Publishers, a division of Main
Line Book Co. All rights reserved. Printed and bound in the United
States of America.

First Printing

1   3   5   7   9   8   6   4   2

Library of Congress Cataloging in Publication Data

La Farge, Ann.
   Gertrude Stein.

   (American women of achievement)
   Bibliography: p.
   Includes index.
   SUMMARY: Traces the life of the American author whose
unique writing style and encouragement of other authors
had a strong influence on culture, particularly in Paris
in the 1920s.
   1. Stein, Gertrude, 1874–1946—Biography—Juvenile
literature.   2. Authors, American—20th century—
Biography—Juvenile literature.   [1. Stein, Gertrude, 1874–
1946.   2. Authors, American]   I. Title.   II. Series.
PS3537.T323Z69   1988   818 '.5209 [B] [92]   87-23929
ISBN 1-55546-678-8

CONTENTS

AMERICAN WOMEN of ACHIEVEMENT

Abigail Adams
women's rights activist

Jane Addams
social worker

Louisa May Alcott
author

Marian Anderson
singer

Susan B. Anthony
woman suffragist

Ethel Barrymore
actress

Clara Barton
*founder of the American
Red Cross*

Elizabeth Blackwell
physician

Nellie Bly
journalist

Margaret Bourke-White
photographer

Pearl Buck
author

Rachel Carson
biologist and author

Mary Cassatt
painter

Agnes De Mille
choreographer

Emily Dickinson
poet

Isadora Duncan
dancer

Amelia Earhart
aviator

Mary Baker Eddy
*founder of the Christian
Science church*

Betty Friedan
feminist

Althea Gibson
tennis champion

Emma Goldman
revolutionary

Helen Hayes
actress

Lillian Hellman
playwright

Katharine Hepburn
actress

Karen Horney
psychoanalyst

Anne Hutchinson
religious leader

Mahalia Jackson
gospel singer

Helen Keller
humanitarian

Jeane Kirkpatrick
diplomat

Emma Lazarus
poet

Clare Boothe Luce
author and diplomat

Barbara McClintock
biologist

Margaret Mead
anthropologist

Edna St. Vincent Millay
poet

Julia Morgan
architect

Grandma Moses
painter

Louise Nevelson
sculptor

Sandra Day O'Connor
Supreme Court Justice

Georgia O'Keeffe
painter

Eleanor Roosevelt
diplomat and humanitarian

Wilma Rudolph
champion athlete

Florence Sabin
physician

Beverly Sills
singer

Gertrude Stein
author

Gloria Steinem
feminist

Harriet Beecher Stowe
author and abolitionist

Mae West
entertainer

Edith Wharton
author

Phillis Wheatley
poet

Babe Zaharias
champion athlete

CHELSEA HOUSE PUBLISHERS

"Remember the Ladies"

MATINA S. HORNER

Remember the Ladies." That is what Abigail Adams wrote to her husband John, then a delegate to the Continental Congress, as the Founding Fathers met in Philadelphia to form a new nation in March of 1776. "Be more generous and favorable to them than your ancestors. Do not put such unlimited power in the hands of the Husbands. If particular care and attention is not paid to the Ladies," Abigail Adams warned, "we are determined to foment a Rebellion, and will not hold ourselves bound by any Laws in which we have no voice, or Representation."

The words of Abigail Adams, one of the earliest American advocates of women's rights, were prophetic. Because when we have not "remembered the ladies," they have, by their words and deeds, reminded us so forcefully of the omission that we cannot fail to remember them. For the history of American women is as interesting and varied as the history of our nation as a whole. American women have played an integral part in founding, settling, and building our country. Some we remember as remarkable women who—against great odds—achieved distinction in the public arena: Anne Hutchinson, who in the 17th century became a charismatic religious leader; Phillis Wheatley, an 18th-century black slave who became a poet; Susan B. Anthony, whose name is synonymous with the 19th-century women's rights movement, and who led the struggle to enfranchise women; and, in our own century, Amelia Earhart, the first woman to cross the Atlantic Ocean by air.

These extraordinary women certainly merit our admiration, but other women, "common women," many of them all but forgotten, should also be recognized for their contributions to American thought and culture. Women have been community builders; they have founded schools and formed voluntary associations to help those in need; they have assumed the major responsibility for rearing children, passing on from one generation to the next the values that keep a culture alive. These and innumerable other contributions, once ignored, are now being recognized by scholars, students, and the public. It is exciting and gratifying to realize that a part of our history that was hardly acknowledged a few generations ago is now being studied and brought to light.

In recent decades, the field of women's history has grown from obscurity to a politically controversial splinter movement to academic respectability, in many cases mainstreamed into such traditional disciplines as history, economics, and psychology. Scholars of women, both female and male, have organized research centers at such prestigious institutions as Wellesley College, Stanford University, and the University of California. Other notable centers for women's studies are the Center for the American Woman and Politics at the Eagleton Institute of Politics at Rutgers University; the Henry A. Murray Research Center for the Study of Lives, at Radcliffe College; and the Women's Research and Education Institute, the research arm of the Congressional Caucus on Women's Issues. Other scholars and public figures have established archives and libraries, such as the Schlesinger Library on the History of Women in America, at Radcliffe College, and the Sophia Smith Collection, at Smith College, to collect and preserve the written and tangible legacies of women.

From the initial donation of the Women's Rights Collection in 1943, the Schlesinger Library grew to encompass vast collections documenting the manifold accomplishments of American women. Simultaneously, the women's movement in general and the academic discipline of women's studies in particular also began with a narrow definition and gradually expanded their mandate. Early causes such as woman suffrage and social reform, abolition and organized labor were joined by newer concerns such as the history of women in business and the professions and in politics and government; the study of the family; and social issues such as health policy and education.

Women, as historian Arthur M. Schlesinger, jr., once pointed out, "have constituted the most spectacular casualty of traditional history. They have made up at least half the human race, but you could never tell that by looking at the books historians write." The new breed of historians is remedying that omission. They have written books about immigrant women and about working-class women who struggled for survival in cities and about black women who met the challenges of life in rural areas. They are telling the stories of women who, despite the barriers of tradition and economics, became lawyers and doctors and public figures.

The women's studies movement has also led scholars to question traditional interpretations of their respective disciplines. For example, the study of war has traditionally been an exercise in military and political analysis, an examination of strategies planned and executed by men. But scholars of women's history have pointed out that wars have also been periods of tremendous change and even opportunity for women, because the very absence of men on the home front enabled them to expand their educational, economic, and professional activities and to assume leadership in their homes.

The early scholars of women's history showed a unique brand of courage in choosing to investigate new subjects and take new approaches to old ones. Often, like their subjects, they endured criticism and even ostracism by their academic colleagues. But their efforts have unquestionably been worthwhile, because with the publication of each new study and book another piece of the historical patchwork is sewn into place, revealing an increasingly comprehensive picture of the role of women in our rich and varied history.

Such books on groups of women are essential, but books that focus on the lives of individuals are equally indispensable. Biographies can be inspirational, offering their readers the example of people with vision who have looked outside themselves for their goals and have often struggled against great obstacles to achieve them. Marian Anderson, for instance, had to overcome racial bigotry in order to perfect her art and perform as a concert singer. Isadora Duncan defied the rules of classical dance to find true artistic freedom. Jane Addams had to break down society's notions of the proper role for women in order to create new social institutions, notably the settlement house. All of these women had to come to terms both with themselves and with the world in which they lived. Only then could they move ahead as pioneers in their chosen callings.

Biography can inspire not only by adulation but also by realism. It helps us see not only the qualities in others that we hope to emulate, but also, perhaps, the weaknesses that made them "human." By helping us identify with the subject on a more personal level they help us to feel that we, too, can achieve such goals. We read about Eleanor Roosevelt, for instance, who occupied a unique and seemingly enviable position as the wife of the president. Yet we can sympathize with her inner dilemma: an inherently shy woman, she had to force herself to live a most public life in order to use her position to benefit others. We may not be able to imagine ourselves having the immense poetic talent of Emily Dickinson, but from her story we can understand the challenges faced by a creative woman who was expected to fulfill many family responsibilities. And though few of us will ever reach the level of athletic accomplishment displayed by Wilma Rudolph or Babe Zaharias, we can still appreciate their spirit, their overwhelming will to excel.

A biography is a multifaceted lens. It is first of all a magnification, the intimate examination of one particular life. But at the same time, it is a wide-angle lens, informing us about the world in which the subject lived. We come away from reading about one life knowing more about the social, political, and economic fabric of the time. It is for this reason, perhaps, that the great New England essayist Ralph Waldo Emerson wrote, in 1841, "There is properly no history: only biography." And it is also why biography, and particularly women's biography, will continue to fascinate writers and readers alike.

GERTRUDE
STEIN

Accompanied by her friend Alice B. Toklas (right), author Gertrude Stein, 60 years old, arrives in the United States for a lecture tour in 1935.

ONE

A Real Lion

When Gertrude Stein arrived in New York City in 1934, she set foot in her native country for the first time in 30 years. The Pennsylvania-born writer had been living in Europe, part of the thriving artistic community there, and had been developing her own unique literary voice. Although she had produced a steady stream of novels, plays, and short stories during that period, her work had been ignored by most of the public. Now, suddenly, she was famous, celebrated for a best-selling book, *The Autobiography of Alice B. Toklas*, and an opera, *Four Saints in Three Acts*, which had opened on Broadway to a roar of critical approval.

Stein, 60 years old when she returned to America, had spent exactly half her life overseas. She had never renounced her native land; "I am American all right," she had said. "Being there does not make me more there." She had, however, promised herself long ago that she would come home only when—and if—she had made a name for herself. "I used to say I would not go to America," she had written, "until I was a real lion and a real celebrity at that time of course I did not really think I was going to be one. But now we were coming and I was going to be one."

As this small sample indicates, Stein's writing style, which was based on the sound and rhythm of words as much as on their meanings, was unusual. A small circle of adventurous readers had long regarded her as a genius, recognizing her as one of the 20th century's most innovative and imaginative writers. Her work, however, had confused most people and had kept the bulk of the reading public away from her books.

Published in 1933, *The Autobiography of Alice B. Toklas* was unlike anything Stein had written before. Its title was misleading—the book was actually the autobiography of Gertrude Stein, not of her lifetime companion, Alice Toklas—but it had been written in a relatively straightforward style. Crammed with comments and anecdotes about famous artists and writers, it provided a fascinating glimpse of Paris during the first quarter of the 20th century and became wildly popular as soon as it rolled off the presses.

Stein and Toklas arrived in New York aboard the ocean liner *Champlain*. When the ship docked, reporters rushed aboard to interview Stein. They were clearly surprised when she responded to their barrage of questions in plain English. Aware that she usually wrote in an obscure, repetitive style, rarely using punctuation, they had expected her to speak in riddles.

"Why don't you write the way you talk?" asked one reporter. "Why don't you read the way I write?" she shot back. Another reporter asked her why she had come to America. "To tell very plainly and simply and directly, as is my fashion," she replied, "what literature is."

The reporters may have been somewhat confused, but they knew good copy when they saw it. In 1934, New York boasted more than a dozen daily newspapers; the day after Stein landed, every one of them featured the story on the front page. Many of the headlines tried to echo Stein's style. One of them read: "Gerty Gerty Stein

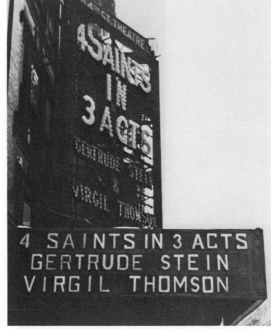

Stein's name blazes from the marquee of New York City's 44th Street Theater. Her opera, Four Saints in Three Acts, *was the smash hit of the 1934 season.*

Is Back Home Home Back." Most of the photographs of Stein showed Toklas hovering in the background; she was described as Stein's "queer, birdlike shadow." Stein, it was noted, wore heavy tweeds, "sensible" shoes, "woolly" stockings, a cherry-colored vest, and a "deerstalker's" cap.

Stein was New York's celebrity of the hour. Wherever she went, cabdrivers smiled and waved, and passersby stared with friendly curiosity. On their first night in the city, Stein and Toklas strolled through Times Square, where they looked up at the lighted sign that circled the *New York Times* building. GERTRUDE STEIN HAS ARRIVED IN NEW YORK, GERTRUDE STEIN HAS ARRIVED IN NEW YORK, proclaimed the lights. Ever since the smash success of *Four Saints in Three Acts*, Stein had been a super-star to New Yorkers.

Four Saints—which was not about four saints and did not have three acts—had an all-black cast and a musical score by American composer Virgil Thomson. It also had a line that would become part of America's popular culture: "the pigeon on the grass alas." The words were part of a song that the public would read aloud, parody, misquote, laugh about—and long remember:

If a magpie in the sky can not cry if the pigeon on the grass alas and to pass the pigeon on the grass alas and the magpie in the sky on the sky and to try and to try alas on the grass alas the pigeon on the grass alas the pigeon on the grass the pigeon on the grass alas and alas.

Stein had come to the United States to give a series of lectures. She spent almost seven months touring the country, speaking at more than 30 universities, visiting almost every state, and becoming reacquainted with her fellow Americans. Her speeches dealt with the two subjects she knew and loved best: art and literature. In one lecture about art, she said, "Everybody must like something, and I like seeing painted pictures.

"Some people," she continued, "like to eat, some people like to drink, some people like to make money, some like to spend money. I have not mentioned games indoor and out, and birds and crime and politics and photography, but anybody can go on, and I, personally, I like all these things well enough but they do not hold my attention long enough. The only thing, funnily enough, that I never get tired of doing is looking at pictures."

Explaining how she felt about modern art, Stein said that the old master-pieces she had seen in the Louvre, Paris's great art museum, had impressed her only as "gold frames which were rather glorious"; on the

Stein (top) and Alice B. Toklas look solemn in their 1934 passport pictures, but they made lively subjects for the reporters who besieged them when they landed in New York City.

15

Toklas (left) and Stein arrive at a Chicago airfield in 1934. Nervous at first about flying, Stein became an enthusiastic air traveler.

comma, she said, "by helping you along holding your coat for you and putting on your shoes keeps you from living your life as actively as you should lead it." She said she thought that stories should not only be told without punctuation; they should be written without a beginning, a middle, or an end. "Only the present moment matters, the visual sense, the texture of that moment," she said.

Like her writing, Stein's lectures intrigued, baffled, and occasionally enraged her audiences. People sometimes got up and walked out while she was speaking, but many more stayed until she finished, fascinated by the large woman with the closely cropped hair and soft, cultured voice that spoke with such passion and simplicity about the things she cared about.

At the end of one lecture, a puzzled man stood up and said he had understood nothing she said; perhaps, he mused, he should have studied more before the lecture. Stein threw up her hands. "You don't need any special preparation to understand," she said impatiently. "A child could understand it. Some children read my work and like it. I like it."

When Stein was not lecturing, she went sightseeing like any other tourist. In New Haven, Connecticut, she and Toklas saw their first football game, a match between Yale and Dartmouth. Stein loved football; it was wonderful,

other hand, she said, the paintings of such modern artists as Henri Matisse and Pablo Picasso had "made the very definite effort to leave their frame."

In another Stein lecture, which dealt with poetry and grammar, she explained why she had always kept punctuation in her writing to a minimum. She said she considered question marks and exclamation marks not only unnecessary but "revolting." She approved of periods because they had "a life of their own," but the use of commas "was positively degrading." A she said, because "nothing happened—it was a spectacle, a landscape, and a ritual, like dancing, war, bullfighting, and theater." Furthermore, a football game, like a good book or a fine painting, had no plot, no narrative drive; it had only what Stein called "moments."

Another new experience for the 60-year-old Stein was an airplane ride. Nervous about flying at first, she soon relaxed, delighted with the view from the airplane. The checkerboard patterns of midwestern fields and forests reminded her, she said, of the paintings of the Cubists, the early 20th-century painters who transformed natural forms into their geometric equivalents.

Chicago—an American phenomenon Stein had never seen—fascinated her. There she and Toklas rode with homicide detectives as they cruised the nighttime city streets, and there she watched a dance marathon. Popular during the Great Depression of the 1930s, marathons were endurance tests for dancers, each of whom hoped to outlast the others and win a cash prize. Stein was intrigued by the marathon dancers, who, she said, "move so strangely and they lead each other about, one asleep completely and the other almost, it is the most unearthly and most beautiful movement I have ever seen."

America abounded with discoveries for the long-absent writer. She eagerly

NBC interviewer William Lundell confers with Toklas (center) and Stein before Stein's 1934 radio debut, which she enjoyed. "It is very nice being a celebrity a real celebrity," she said.

read her first comic book, devoured her first serving of oysters Rockefeller (oysters baked with spinach), and, with wide-eyed amazement, visited her first modern American drugstore. Always enthusiastic about cars (in France, she was the proud owner of a Ford), she drove one whenever she got the chance. "The romantic thing about America," she said later, was that "they do the best designing and use the best material in the cheapest thing, the [comic] books and the old Ford car." Some witnesses observed that Stein's driving resembled her writing; it was unpunctuated with stops. As one friend put it, "She regarded a corner as something to cut, and another car as something to pass, and she could scare the daylights out of all concerned."

Stein said that when she looked down from an airplane, she "saw all the lines of Cubism." The view reminded her of paintings like this one, Pablo Picasso's 1909 work, The Reservoir.

Behaving like any other tourist in California, Stein poses with a cross-section from an ancient sequoia tree. Its rings are labeled with the historical events that took place during its growth.

Stein visited schools, factories, bookshops, theaters, restaurants, and department stores. In California, she had dinner with her favorite actor, comedian Charlie Chaplin, and in Washington, D.C., she was invited to the White House. Of this occasion, Stein reported, "Mrs. [Eleanor] Roosevelt was there and gave us tea. She talked about something and we sat next to some one."

She met many of America's foremost writers, including Dashiell Hammett, whose detective stories she enjoyed. How was it, someone asked her, that she liked such fiction, which met none of her criteria for literature? She gave one of her typical explanations: "The hero is dead to begin with and so you have so to speak got rid of the event before the book begins."

What Stein most enjoyed about her visit to the United States was her discussions with the college students who crowded her lectures. Young people responded to her, and she to them; her talks were always followed by lively question-and-answer sessions. At one, a student asked her to explain one of her most frequently quoted lines, "Rose is a rose is a rose is a rose."

Stein, who had announced on her arrival that she had come to America to explain "what literature is," responded gleefully. "You have seen hundreds of poems about roses and you know in your bones the rose is not there," she said. "Now listen! I'm no fool; I know that in daily life we don't go around saying, 'is a.... is.... is....' Yes, I'm no fool; but I think that in that line, the rose is red for the first time in English poetry for a hundred years."

After attending one of Stein's lectures, a student—sounding himself a little like Stein—wrote in his college newspaper: "I was dead against her and I just went to see what she looked like and then she took the door of my mind right off its hinges and now it's wide open." Such a reaction did not surprise Stein. "Why they talk to me," she said of her student audiences, "is that I am like them, I do not know the answer.... I do not even know whether there is a question let alone having an answer for a question."

Stein and Toklas traveled through New England, the South, Texas, the Midwest, and to the Pacific Coast. At the end of their tour, they visited Oakland, California, where Stein had spent much of her childhood. The city had changed little since she lived there, but she felt no sense of homecoming, no nostalgia, no emotional connection with her old hometown. Later, she wrote, "That's what makes your identity, not a thing that exists but something you do or do not remember." History, for Stein, was not merely a record of events; it was a story to be imagined, even invented. "Our roots can be anywhere and we can survive because, if you think about it, we take our roots with us," she wrote.

Stein had taken her roots to Paris, and after more than six months in America, she knew it was time to return to them. She had always yearned for *la gloire*—glory—dreaming of recognition as a literary "lion," and now she had it. In America, she had been listened to, stared at, interviewed, quoted, and endlessly photographed. Her opera had been a smash hit and her book a best-seller. Her opinion had been sought on everything from politics (she was a staunchly conservative Republican) to food (she wished there were more varieties of pie).

Accompanied by Alice B. Toklas, Gertrude Stein left the United States on May 4, 1935. "We've seen everything," she told reporters. "We've seen it from the air, and we've seen it from the ground and in all kinds of ways, and in every way we've found it completely fascinating." Stein would grow even more famous in her native land, but she would never see it again.

Gertrude, whom her father had called "a perfect baby," is shown here at age three or four. The future author spent her early childhood years in Vienna, Austria.

TWO

A Young American

When the Stein family—Michael, Hanne, and their five sons—emigrated from Germany to the United States in 1841, they opened a clothing store in Baltimore, Maryland. In 1862, two of the Steins' sons, 29-year-old Daniel and his younger brother Solomon, moved to Pittsburgh, Pennsylvania, where they established their own store, Stein Brothers. Daniel soon met and fell in love with Amelia Keyser, a 21-year-old woman whose parents had also come to America from Germany. Even before they married in 1864, Daniel and Amelia had decided on the size of their family: They wanted five children, no more, no less.

Their first child, Michael, was born in 1865; Simon arrived in 1867, and Bertha three years later. Sadly, the Steins' fourth and fifth babies died in infancy, but Leo, a fine, healthy boy, was born in 1872. He was followed in 1874 by Gertrude, who was, said her father, "a perfect baby." As they were growing up, Leo and Gertrude often reminded each other how lucky they were to have been born, thinking of themselves as replacements for the children who had not survived. They became inseparable companions.

Daniel and Solomon Stein were neighbors as well as business partners—they lived next door to each other in the Pittsburgh suburb of Allegheny—but relations between the two families were strained. The brothers frequently disagreed about how their store should be run, and their wives quarreled constantly. In 1875, Amelia and Daniel Stein decided to move to Vienna, Austria, where Daniel planned to start a new business.

Gertrude was less than one year old when she left the country of her birth; she would not return for more than five years. She later remembered her early childhood in Vienna as a happy time; she could run and play as she pleased in her family's big, comfortable house and in the city's large parks; there were dancing lessons, horseback rides, elaborate picnics, and huge, delicious meals prepared by her mother's cook.

As the baby of the family, Gertrude was coddled and indulged by her parents, her siblings, and her Aunt Rachel, who lived with the Steins in Vienna. After Daniel Stein returned to the United States to start yet another new business, Rachel Keyser wrote to him about his youngest child. "Our little Gertie," she said, "is a little Schnatterer [chatterbox]. She talks all day long, and so plainly. *She outdoes them all.*"

Gertrude had come, very early in life, to enjoy being the center of attention. Many years later she wrote, "One should always be the youngest member of the family. It saves you a lot of bother, everybody takes care of you, that is the way I was and that is the way I still am and anyone who is like that necessarily liked it. I did and I do."

Just before Gertrude's fifth birthday, the Steins decided to spend a year in Paris and then go back to the United States. Gertrude had been speaking German for four years; now she learned to "schnatter" in French. She also learned to enjoy shopping, one of her mother's favorite pastimes. Mother and daughter went on a memorable shopping spree before they sailed for America. Stein later recalled that they

Amelia and Daniel Stein, Gertrude's parents, shared the same German-Jewish heritage. Amelia had been born in the United States, and Daniel had immigrated with his family.

"bought everything that pleased their fancy, seal skin coats and caps and muffs for the whole family from the mother to the small sister Gertrude Stein, gloves dozens of gloves, wonderful hats, riding costumes, and finally ending up with a microscope and a whole set of famous french history of zoology." Stein grew up to be an intellectual and a serious artist, but she never outgrew her childlike pleasure in shopping.

In Vienna, Gertrude got her first taste of books—"picture books, but books all the same," she later recalled.

Arriving in the United States in 1879, the Steins spent a few months with Amelia Stein's family in Baltimore. Here Gertrude learned English, and here, as she said later, her "emotions began to feel themselves in English." No matter where she lived in later years, Stein always wrote exclusively in English, and she always identified herself as an American.

In 1880, Daniel Stein decided to move his family again, this time to California, a young state (it had joined the union in 1850) where business prospects looked promising. Six-year-old Gertrude—whose recollections almost always included food—said that what she remembered about the long railroad trip to the West Coast was "landscape as well as eating and moving."

Daniel Stein took a job with San Francisco's Omnibus Cable Company, which built and operated the cable

Gertrude's brother Leo Stein leans on a pillow in this 1877 family portrait, made in Vienna. Standing (left to right) with their governess and tutor are Gertrude and siblings: Bertha, Simon, and Michael.

cars that carried (and continue to carry) passengers up the city's extremely steep hills. He settled his family in a big house in East Oakland, on the outskirts of San Francisco. For Gertrude and Leo, East Oakland was paradise. Situated on 10 acres of sunny, rolling land, their house was surrounded by overgrown lawns, apple and cherry trees, and thickets of wild roses.

In her 1925 novel *The Making of Americans*, Stein recalled the joyous summer days she and her brother spent in California. "It was very pleasant then," she wrote, "lying there watching the birds, black in the bright sunlight and sailing, and the firm white summer clouds breaking away from the horizon and slowly moving. . . . In the summer it was good. . . . to fill one's hat with fruit and sit on the dry ploughed ground and eat and think and sleep and read and dream and never hear them when they would all be calling."

The young Steins were equally delighted with the California autumns, when, wrote Gertrude, "the wind would be so strong it would blow the leaves and branches of the trees down.... and you could shout and work and get wet and be all soaking and run out full into the strong wind and let it dry you, in between the gusts of rain that left you soaking. It was fun all the things that happened all the year there then."

Life had many pleasures for Gertrude during these years. "Most of all," she once recalled, "there were books and food, food and books, both excellent things." She and Leo shared a passion for books. Together, they read all of Shakespeare's plays, the works of Wordsworth and other English poets, 18th- and 19th-century novels, biographies, histories, scientific handbooks, and encyclopedias. Whenever they had a chance, the two also saw local theater productions and performances by visiting opera and drama companies.

Neither Gertrude nor Leo made many friends in school, Leo because he was painfully shy and Gertrude because she was perfectly satisfied with Leo's company. Having an older brother, she wrote later, "makes everything a pleasure to you, you go everywhere and do everything while he does it all for you and with you which is a pleasant way to have everything happen to you."

In this photograph, four-year-old Gertrude assumes an uncharacteristically serious expression. A lively child, she was known as the family schnatterer, *or chatterbox.*

25

Except for their brother Michael, Gertrude and Leo were indifferent to the other members of their family. Serious and kind, Michael respected his bright siblings and did his best to share their enthusiasms, but he was much older than they were and less intellectually inclined. "He used to make nice little jokes too that pleased us," Gertrude would later write, "and Leo and I always liked giving him a book to read, he never read any book except one that we gave him and that he always read from the beginning to the ending. He always had these pleasant little ways." With affectionate amusement, she recalled the day she and Leo brought home a copy of a painting they admired, Jean-François Millet's *Man with a Hoe*, which they had seen in a San Francisco art gallery. Michael examined it solemnly and then gave his opinion: "It is a hell of a hoe."

Leo and Gertrude had no use for their sister, Bertha, or their brother Simon. "It is not natural to care about a sister," Gertrude once wrote, "certainly not when she is four years older and grinds her teeth at night." They considered Simon, who may have been somewhat retarded, as too fat and "funny" to bother with. They also found their parents unappealing. Daniel Stein, who had been made vice-president of the Omnibus Cable Company, was often away from home, but when he was there, he made stern, often conflicting household rules that his children deeply resented.

Leo later called his father "a stocky, positive, dominant, aggressive person, with no book learning whatever." Gertrude recalled him as "depressing." The young people were fond of their mother, although in a somewhat patronizing way. In *The Making of Americans*, Gertrude Stein wrote of her family, "The little mother was not very important to them. They were good enough children in their daily living but they were never very loving to her inside them." Gertrude did concede that her mother "had a gentle little bounty in her" and that she dressed well, usually wearing "pleasant stuffs for children to rub against."

Amelia Stein, whose health had begun to fail soon after her arrival in California, had become an invalid by 1886. After her long illness, her death from cancer in 1888 seems to have made little impression on 14-year-old Gertrude. "We had all already had the habit of doing without her," she noted calmly.

When Daniel Stein took over the running of the household, Gertrude and Leo grew closer to each other and even more distant from the rest of the family. They particularly avoided their father, whose discipline and regulations they found oppressive. He had become, said his daughter, even "more of a bother than he had been."

For the rest of her life, Gertrude

A Union Pacific locomotive pulls passenger cars westward in the 1870s. When the Steins moved from Baltimore, Maryland, to Oakland, California, in 1880, they rode a similar train.

Stein would deeply resent all authority figures. According to some scholars and psychologists, this attitude was rooted in her antipathy toward her father. "Hitherto we had naturally not had to remember him most of the time," she wrote of the period following her mother's death, "and now remembering him had begun."

At the age of 14, Gertrude entered what she later called "the agony of adolescence." She described this period as one where everything "is really medieval and pioneer and nothing is clear and nothing is sure, and nothing is safe and nothing is come and nothing is gone." Not even the company of Leo made up for the insecurity she

The city hall clock tower dominates the low skyline of Oakland, California, in the 1880s. The Steins lived on a small farm on the outskirts of the city.

was feeling; despite their almost endless conversations about books and paintings, the two rarely discussed their emotions. As Leo wrote many years later, "Gertrude and I despite constant companionship throughout our childhood and early youth. . . . never said a word to each other about our inner life."

Like many teenagers, Stein discovered not only loneliness and alienation but boredom. "A great deal of time," she wrote later, "there is nothing to do except stand around in games and in the evening and in the day, stand around, not even get up and sit down but just stand around." Life for Ger-

trude, her sister, and her brothers, however, changed radically in 1891.

In *Everybody's Autobiography*, published in 1937, Stein wrote about that year, when she was 17: "Then one morning we could not wake up our father. Leo climbed in by the window and called out to us that he was dead in bed and he was." Never given to false sentimentality, she added, "Then our life without a father began a very pleasant one."

Twenty-six-year-old Michael now took charge of his brothers and sisters, bringing them to his own house in San Francisco. Becoming the legal guardian of Leo and Gertrude, who were still minors, Michael set to work sorting out his father's affairs. "There were so many debts," recalled Gertrude later, "it was frightening, and then I found out that profit and loss is always loss." Michael, who was working as manager of the Omnibus Cable Company, was a solid, practical young man; he managed to pay his father's debts, sell his stocks and properties, and reinvest it to produce enough money for all the Stein siblings to live on for the rest of their lives. "How it was done," said Gertrude later, "nobody ever knew," but the income provided by her brother's investments turned out to be enough to keep the family "reasonably poor."

Leo and Gertrude, who would become prominent art collectors, in childhood purchased a copy of Jean-François Millet's widely admired 1863 painting, Man with a Hoe.

The Stein family gathers for a musical evening in Oakland. From left to right are Simon, Daniel, Gertrude (at her father's feet), Michael, Amelia, Leo, and Bertha.

Both Leo and Gertrude had dropped out of high school before their father died. Leo, as his sister recalled, had done "three years' high school work in seven months" and entered the University of California. Gertrude, who had detested school, had also continued her studies at home. Although she never got a high school diploma, by the time she was 18 years old, she was a reasonably well educated young woman.

In 1891, Leo was accepted as an undergraduate at Harvard College in Cambridge, Massachusetts. Because Michael had decided his sisters would be better off living with their mother's family in Baltimore, he sent them East with Leo. Gertrude was no fonder of Bertha than ever, but she loved living in Baltimore with her mother's sister, Fanny Bachrach, and her extended family. Here, she wrote later, she "began to lose her lonesomeness" and to exchange the "rather desperate inner life" she had been living in California with the "cheerful life" of her aunts and uncles.

There was, however, one big problem: Gertrude missed Leo terribly. In the winter of her 18th year, she visited him at Harvard, where the air itself seemed to crackle with intellectual energy. Leo and his fellow students talked with great animation about their philosophy courses, particularly those taught by William James, the leading light of a new branch of philosophy called psychology. They were wildly excited about James's recent book, *The Principles of Psychology*, which had electrified the entire American scholarly community.

Harvard attracted the brightest minds in the country. It was a hotbed of new ideas and educational experiments, and some of its faculty had begun teaching women at a separate institution known as the Harvard Annex since 1879. In 1894 the Annex was chartered as Radcliffe College, formally affiliated with Harvard University. Gertrude Stein knew she belonged there. In the autumn of 1893, she enrolled at the Harvard Annex as a philosophy student.

Dressed up for a formal portrait in 1895, college student Stein wears an outfit with fashionable "leg-of-mutton" sleeves. Her everyday attire was much more casual.

THREE

College Years

Gertrude Stein, "having become more humanized and less adolescent and less lonesome," as she put it in *The Autobiography of Alice B. Toklas*, "went to Radcliffe. There she had a very good time." As soon as she arrived in Cambridge, she settled into the boardinghouse that would be her home for the next four years.

She found her fellow boarders unlike anyone she had met so far ("Everyone," she wrote later, "was New England there"), but she liked them. They liked her, too, despite her unconventional ways of talking and dressing. The other young women at Harvard piled their long hair into fashionable pompadours, encased themselves in boned corsets, and wore tightly buttoned, high-collared dresses and lace-up boots. Stein, who was quite heavy, dressed for comfort, as she would continue to do all her life. She pulled her hair tightly back from her face, dis-

dained corsets, and wore loose dark-colored dresses and flat-heeled shoes or sandals.

Stein loved to walk. With friends from her boardinghouse, she often rode to the end of the trolley-car line and took long hikes in the country. Well-brought-up young women of the time were expected to have male protection when they ventured away from home, but Stein's friends counted on her for safety. Recalling her walks with Stein, one classmate later reminisced with amusement: "We said if we have any trouble with a man, Gertrude will climb out on the furthest limb of a tree and drop on him." Stein was also fond of bicycling; she was often seen around Cambridge, her skirts flapping, her unstockinged legs pedaling furiously.

Because she had never graduated from high school, Stein was enrolled as a "special student," but she took the same classes as everyone else and was

Students and their families stroll in Harvard Yard after a graduation ceremony in the 1890s. Stein, who failed her final examination in Latin, left Radcliffe in 1897 without a degree.

treated in the same way by her teachers. Following in Leo's footsteps, she signed up for courses with the eminent philosophers George Santayana and Josiah Royce and with psychologist-philosopher William James. She also took English composition, zoology, and botany as well as required courses in mathematics, physics, and chemistry. She enjoyed and did well in philosophy and writing but was an average science student.

Most of the pieces Stein wrote for her composition class were intensely personal. One was about a young woman—not unlike herself—who sits in a library, thinking about her life. "Books, books, is there no end to it. Nothing but myself to feed my own eager nature. Nothing given to me but musty books," wrote the 18-year-old Stein.

Her writing teacher, poet and playwright William Vaughn Moody (who later earned literary fame for such plays as *The Faith Healer*), found her work original but careless. It was, he said, "not without psychological interest," and it showed "considerable emotional intensity and a somewhat unusual power of abstract thought." However, said Moody, it was "frequently lacking in organization. . . . and in artfulness of literary method." Voicing a criticism of Stein's writing that would be often heard in later years, Moody added, "I wish you might overcome your disdain for the more necessary marks of punctuation."

Among the essays Stein wrote for Moody was one in which she expressed her devotion to William James. "Is life worth living?" she asked rhetorically. "Yes, a thousand times yes when the world still holds such spirits as Prof. James. He is truly a man among men." James, famous for his massive work, *The Principles of Psychology*, was also celebrated for his unique skills as a teacher. Restless, brilliant, and innovative, he liked young people and was always ready to listen to them talk. He was willing to accept unconventional ideas, insisting that any possible truth had to be taken seriously. Not surprisingly, he found Gertrude Stein's lively and unconventional mind appealing; she, in turn, was deeply influenced by him.

James, who coined the phrase "stream of consciousness," often talked about the way in which the human mind perceived time. He asserted that it viewed past, present, and future as a single entity. This concept impressed Stein, who later adopted a style known as the "continuous present" in her writing. James, Stein said many years later, "was my big influence when I was at college. He

Harvard professor William James, author of The Principles of Psychology, *liked and respected Stein. The feeling was mutual: she called him "truly a man among men."*

was a man who always said 'complicate your life as much as you please, it has got to simplify.' "

Among the many subjects that intrigued William James was "automatic writing," in which a subject writes messages, possibly from the subconscious mind, while in a trance. Stein took part in a number of automatic-writing experiments under James's supervision; the paper she wrote about the phenomenon was printed in the Harvard *Psychological Review* in 1896. Entitled "Normal Motor Automatism," it was her first published work. James, highly pleased with his star pupil's progress, invited her to attend his ad-

Gertrude and Leo Stein link arms after a tennis match at Harvard. Two years apart in age, brother and sister were inseparable companions for much of their lives.

vanced seminars, a high honor for an undergraduate.

James's affectionate respect for Stein was made clear one spring day when she showed up for a final examination for one of his courses. According to *The Autobiography of Alice B. Toklas*, "She sat down with the examination paper before her and she just could not. Dear Professor James, she wrote at the top of her paper. I am so sorry but really I do not feel a bit like an examination paper in philosophy today, and left."

The following day, reported Stein, "she had a postal card from William James saying, Dear Miss Stein, I understand perfectly how you feel I often feel like that myself. And underneath it he gave her work the highest mark in his course."

Stein studied hard at Radcliffe, but she also had an active social life, and she took part in a variety of extracurricular activities. She was secretary of the Philosophy Club and a member of the Idler Club, a campus dramatic group. With Leo and his friends, she often went to the opera and the theater, to Boston Symphony concerts and art galleries, and on picnics and hikes. She was a frequent participant in heated all-night talk sessions in which the subjects ranged from art to religion to politics.

In 1895, when Leo Stein graduated from Harvard and left for a world tour, his sister began to think about her own future. After discussing it with William James, she decided to become a psychologist. This, said James, would require a medical education. And before she could enter medical school, she would need a degree from Radcliffe—which, in turn, meant learning Latin, then required of all graduates. Stein, who had never studied the ancient language, hired a tutor, but Latin bored her, and she paid little attention to her lessons. As a result, she failed her final examination and was denied her degree for the time being.

Stein wanted to work for her medical degree at Baltimore's Johns Hopkins

Horse-drawn vehicles roll across Harvard Square in the 1890s. The prim manners of New Englanders made California-bred Stein feel like a foreigner at first, but she adjusted quickly.

University School of Medicine, which had recently begun to admit women. Here she could be near her aunts and uncles, and here she could be reunited with Leo, who was already registered at the university as a graduate student in biology. Despite her lack of a Har-vard degree, Stein was accepted at Johns Hopkins, largely at the urging of William James, who believed she had a brilliant future in psychology. Admitted to the Baltimore institution in the fall of 1897, she was awarded her Harvard degree the following spring.

Stein (center) appears in a play presented by the Idler's Club, Harvard's amateur dramatic society. More mature-looking than most of her classmates, she was often cast as an older woman.

In the late 19th century, many people considered medical school a strange place for a young woman to be. Most of Stein's fellow Radcliffe students had put their intellectual lives behind them when they left college, pursuing instead the roles of wife and mother. "My dear Gertrude," wrote one old friend, "I will say in a word that a sheltered life, domestic tastes, maternity, and faith are all I could ask for myself or you or the great mass of womankind. I overworked and overreached—too much ambition, too little faith in traditional ideals. . . . When you begin possibly to waver in 'being a useful member of society' . . . you may recall my experience and my affectionate advice."

When Michael Stein's wife, who had a two-year old son, heard of her sister-in-law's plan to enter medical school, she, too, wrote her a letter. "There is certainly nothing in the line of happiness to compare with that which a mother derives from the contemplation of her first-born," said Sally Stein, "and even the agony which she endures from the moment of its birth does not seem to mar it, therefore my dear and beloved sister-in-law, go and get married."

The concept of equality for women was beginning to blossom in the 1890s, but Gertrude Stein was not part of the contemporary women's movement. She would, in fact, soon write, "I am for having women learn what they can but not to. . . . believe that a man's work is suited to them because they have mastered a boy's education."

Although she was not a feminist, Stein was fiercely committed to her own independence, and she had no intention of letting anyone push her into a life she did not want. What she did not want was "a sheltered life, domestic tastes, and maternity." She wanted education, more opportunities to stretch her mind, good books, and good company.

In the fall of 1897, Gertrude and Leo Stein rented a house in Baltimore, hired a German housekeeper named Lena Lebender, and settled down to their studies. Lebender took firm

Gertrude (under "X") and Leo Stein (to left of mast) join a group of college friends for a cruise aboard the Vigilant *in July 1897.*

charge of both the household and "Miss Gertrude." Ten years later, Stein would recreate this period of her life in "The Good Anna," one of the trio of novellas that composed her 1908 book *Three Lives*.

"The Good Anna" is based on Lebender; Miss Mathilda, another character in the story, is modeled on Stein herself. Overweight and extravagant, Miss Mathilda is constantly chided by Anna for buying too many paintings and theater tickets. "And I slave and slave to save the money," complains the housekeeper, "and you go out and spend it all on foolishness." The story was a fairly accurate reflection of life as it was: Lebender often scolded her young mistress for spending her allowance too freely, dressing carelessly, and neglecting her studies.

Gertrude and Leo Stein spent most of their free time visiting Baltimore's museums and galleries and visiting the homes of intellectual and artistic friends. Among this circle were Etta and Claribel Cone, wealthy Baltimore sisters who held well-attended Saturday night "evenings" at which Leo Stein often made long speeches about paintings, etchings, and Japanese prints.

Dr. Claribel Cone, outspoken, independent, and somewhat domineering, had graduated from Johns Hopkins in 1891; Etta Cone, shy, patient, and sensitive, waited on her older sister almost like a servant. Inspired by the Steins'

Sally Stein (left) and her son Allan hold hands with Gertrude Stein in 1899. Disapproving of her sister-in-law's lifestyle, Sally urged her to marry and have children.

passionate interest in art, the Cones began to acquire valuable prints and paintings. Eventually becoming important collectors, they would continue to cross paths with Gertrude and Leo Stein in the years to come.

By 1900, Leo Stein decided he had spent enough time at Johns Hopkins. "I had soon realized," he later wrote, "that I could do nothing in a laboratory, and one day I got a great idea in aesthetics.... and I dropped biology and decided to go to Florence [Italy] for a few years." Left alone in Baltimore, Gertrude Stein began drifting toward a new set of friends.

The group she fell in with was known as "fast"; they were rebellious college-educated women who met regularly to discuss their views of society and its problems. Rejecting the strait-laced moral codes of the 1890s, these women insisted on their right to live their lives as they saw fit. They proclaimed "female superiority," disdained conventional religious and political beliefs, and openly discussed the lesbianism that many of them practiced.

Stein was strongly attracted by the long discussions, the festive group outings, and the open, easygoing way in

Holding up a clue, Leo Stein (center) faces his sister during a treasure hunt with friends at Quisset, Massachusetts, in the summer of 1897.

Stein peers into a laboratory microscope at Johns Hopkins University School of Medicine. Medical school bored Stein; after three years, she left without graduating.

which these young women interacted. The group warmly welcomed the bright, unconventional Stein. Then, "with all the eagerness of a new convert," writes one of her biographers, Janet Hobhouse, "she embraced its doctrines and fell in love."

May Bookstaver, the intelligent and beautiful young woman with whom Stein became infatuated, returned her affection, but she was already romantically involved with someone else. The three-year relationship between the two women was a heartbreaking experience for Stein, who fictionalized it in a novel, *Q.E.D. Q.E.D.* stands for *quod erat demonstrandum*, a Latin phrase that means, roughly translated, "what has been proven."

The central characters in *Q.E.D.* are Adele, modeled on the author, and Helen, based on May Bookstaver. Helen, described as the "American version of the English handsome girl," belongs to a crowd of women who reject society's conventional rules and do not attempt to hide their homosexuality. She criticizes straitlaced Adele's middle-class views. "You are so afraid of losing your moral sense," she tells her, "that you are not willing to take it through anything more dangerous than a mud-puddle."

Tormented by Helen's disapproval, Adele is also torn between her need for "a love that can tear down the walls that enclose her and let her escape into a world of humans" and her desire for a life of "obvious, superficial, clean simplicity." At the end of the novel, Adele leaves Helen and her friends and returns to conventional values. She comes to the conclusion "that the middle-class ideal which demands that people be affectionate, respectable, honest, and content, that they avoid excitements and cultivate serenity, is the ideal that appeals to me." With these words, Stein outlined a philosophy she would follow for the rest of her life.

She finished *Q.E.D.* in 1903, three years before Bookstaver married a man named Charles Knoblauch in a fashionable Newport, Rhode Island, wedding. Stein referred briefly to *Q.E.D.* in *The Autobiography of Alice B. Toklas*: "The funny thing about this short novel," she wrote, "is that she [Stein] completely forgot about it for many years.... She must have forgotten about it almost immediately." Stein never published the book, which appeared after her death under the title *Things as They Are*.

Concerned about Stein's association with her new, "fast" crowd and about her recent preoccupation with her health, friends wrote to her brother in Florence. They told him that Gertrude, who had decided that her blood was "weak," had designed a unique form of therapy: She had hired a boxer to spar with her. A friend who had a room beneath Stein's later recalled, "The chandelier in my room used to swing, and the house echoed with shouts of 'Now give me one on the jaw! Now give me one in the kidney!'"

When reports of his sister's activities reached Leo Stein in early 1903, he quickly dispatched a letter to Baltimore. "What is all this nonmedicated rumble that issues from your quarter?" he asked. Then, suspecting that she was planning to drop her medical studies, he added, "It would be too bad if the first person in the family

Claribel (left) and Etta Cone (right) share a table with Stein in Florence, Italy, in 1903. Inspired by Stein and her brother, the wealthy Cone sisters became avid art collectors.

who had gone so far as to get the adequate preparation for anything should go back on it. Well, I suppose you won't."

Stein, who was planning to do exactly what her brother feared she would, summarized her four years of medical school in *The Autobiography of Alice B. Toklas*. The "first two years Gertrude Stein liked well enough," she wrote. "She always liked knowing a lot of people and being mixed up in a lot of stories and she was not awfully interested but she was not too bored with what she was doing and besides she had quantities of pleasant relatives in Baltimore and she liked it." For two years, she received excellent grades.

The second two years were another story. "She was bored, frankly openly bored," wrote Stein of herself. "The practice and theory of medicine did not interest her at all." Stein had begun to doodle and daydream through her classes, and her grades had plummeted. Her professors were distressed; she had come to Johns Hopkins with a reputation for being William James's favorite pupil and for doing brilliant and original work, and now she was behaving like a mediocre student. More and more, when she was called on in class, she simply said she did not know the answers.

Some of Stein's teachers gave her passing grades despite her obvious lack of interest; others tried to teach her a lesson by giving her the poor grades her work deserved. When she finally failed a crucial examination, one of her friends pleaded with her to study and take the test again. "Gertrude, Gertrude, remember the cause of women!" entreated the friend. But it was impossible to teach Stein a lesson she did not want to learn, and "the cause of women," as she once said, did "not happen to be her business." To her friend, she simply replied, "You don't know what it is to be bored."

The professor whose final examination Stein had failed in the spring of 1901 offered her the chance to go to summer school and get her medical degree in the fall. To his astonishment, she not only refused his offer; she thanked him for failing her. "You have no idea how grateful I am to you," she said. "If you had not kept me from taking my degree I would have, well,

Stein (top left) joins a group of fellow medical students in Baltimore. She "wasn't easy to know," said one of her classmates, "but once you knew her, you found her to be charming."

not taken to the practice of medicine, but at any rate to pathological psychology and you don't know how little I like pathological psychology, and how all medicine bores me." And that, she reported, "was the end of the medical education of Gertrude Stein."

Stein is flanked by her brothers, Leo (left) and Michael, in Paris. The three siblings, who had always gotten along well, called themselves "The Stein Corporation."

FOUR

"Endlessly the Same and Endlessly Different"

Gertrude Stein, who would spend the next three years shuttling between Europe and the United States, joined her brother in England in 1901. The brilliant, articulate Leo Stein had made many friends among Europe's intellectual elite; through him, Gertrude Stein met some of the era's most celebrated literary and artistic figures. Surrounded by people who spent much of their time discussing painting, architecture, music, and philosophy, Stein remained enthusiastic, direct, and more than willing to share her ideas.

A "lady" of the early 20th century was expected to be fashionably dressed, reserved, and soft-spoken, but Stein had never had much use for convention. She continued to wear her customary voluminous, dark-colored dresses and cheerfully vented her opinions about everything from art to politics. Unlike many Americans living in England, Stein refused to make un-

flattering comparisons between the cultural climate of her homeland and the highly civilized atmosphere of Europe. On the contrary, she missed no opportunity to praise the United States, making it her practice, as her brother noted later, "to blow the American trumpet."

In the fall of 1903, Stein decided to move in with her brother, who had rented an apartment in Paris. At the time, she expected to make annual trips back to the United States, but except for a visit to New York City in the winter of 1903–1904, she would remain in Europe for more than 30 years.

In 1904, Stein wrote that, for Americans, "it is a common experience that our youth extends through the whole first 29 years of our life and it is not until we reach 30 that we find at last that vocation for which we feel ourselves fit and to which we willingly devote labor." One of her friends once recalled that "as early as 1900, Gertrude was most outspoken about wanting glory from life.... She repeated it again and again: 'la gloire.' "

When she was 30, Stein decided that she would attain "la gloire" through writing. She had already written a novel, *Q.E.D.*, and a short story, "Fernhurst," both as yet unpublished, both written in a fairly conventional style. In 1903 she had written the first draft of a long novel called *The Making of Americans*, which, when it was published in 1925, would demonstrate the new, unorthodox style for which she became celebrated.

Ever since she had studied psychology with William James at Harvard, Stein had been developing her own theory about people's similarities and differences. After carefully considering the reactions of students she had watched participating in James's experiments with automatic writing, she had decided that people could be classified. Each individual, she thought, belonged to one of a small number of types; the way that individual reacted to circumstances and stresses defined his or her "bottom nature," or distinct personality. "I finally felt," she wrote in *Everybody's Autobiography*, "that one could make diagrams and describe every individual man and woman who ever was or is or will be living."

Living in Paris with her brother, Stein met scores of stimulating new people;

she began to take notes about them, recording and classifying their "bottom natures." To acquire knowledge of others, she wrote later, a writer needed "to be able to talk and listen to listen while talking and talk while listening." Following her own theories, she began to write *Three Lives*, which, when it appeared in 1909, would be her first published work of fiction.

Three Lives contains "The Good Anna," Stein's portrait of her Baltimore

Art expert Bernard Berenson studies a rare drawing. It was at Berenson's suggestion that Leo Stein bought his first "modern art," a painting by the brilliant Paul Cézanne.

Pedestrians, carriages, and horse-powered buses crowd Paris's Montmartre Boulevard in 1901, the year that Gertrude Stein moved into her brother's apartment at 27 rue de Fleurus.

housekeeper; "The Gentle Lena," also about a servant; and "Melanctha," the story of a passionate young black woman and her quiet, hardworking lover. "Melanctha," the longest of the three stories, is also the best known and most widely read of all Stein's work.

The first American fiction to present black people as individuals rather than as racial stereotypes, "Melanctha" is also notable for its dialogue. Stein believed that people revealed themselves through their repeated actions. The best way for a writer to express those revelations, she decided, was through repetition in speech. Her characters do not speak in realistic language. Instead, as critic Michael J. Hoffman points out in his 1976 book, *Gertrude*

Cézanne, whose experiments in form and color would help shape the abstract art of the future, painted this self-portrait. His work formed the nucleus of the Steins' art collection.

Stein, "Stein lets her characters talk in long, stylized, repetitious speeches, [which] present the reader with a symbolic sense of [the characters'] innermost natures."

Stein herself explained it this way: "I began to get enormously interested in hearing how everybody said the same thing over and over again ... until finally if you listened with great intensity you could ... tell all that there was inside them, not so much by the actual words they said ... but the movement of their thoughts and words endlessly the same and endlessly different."

In "Melanctha," Stein introduced a literary device that came to be known as the "continuous present." Instead of telling her story in a straight narrative line from past to present to future, she reports it in a series of discrete moments, each of which is in the present. At the core of "Melanctha," notes Hoffman, is "process *within* a moment rather than process from moment to moment." Stein's works, says Hoffman, are "highly unified because she concentrates in each separate moment upon the same set of qualities that defines the basic natures of her characters."

In the early 20th century, Paris was about to witness a creative explosion that would revolutionize the history of art. Leo and Gertrude Stein's apartment at 27 rue de Fleurus gradually became a kind of headquarters for the artists who would spark that explosion; indeed, the Steins themselves would play a major part in it.

Although brother and sister had been buying prints and replicas of well-known sculptures for years, it was not until 1903 that Leo Stein bought his first original painting, a landscape by British artist Wilson Steer. Buying it, Leo said later, made him feel "a bit like a desperado. Oil paintings were for the rich." Now, he said, he realized that "one could actually own paintings even if one were not a millionaire."

Leo Stein's next purchase was made after a conversation with his friend

Bernard Berenson, a distinguished art critic, historian, and collector. Stein, who reported the dialogue in his autobiography, complained to Berenson that there was a "dearth of art" in Paris. "Do you know Cézanne?" asked Berenson. Stein said he had never heard of him and asked where he could see his work. "At Vollard's," said Berenson. "I went to Vollard's," recalled Stein, "and was launched."

This dialogue, which Gertrude Stein biographer Janet Hobhouse calls "one of the most important exchanges in the history of art collecting," resulted in Leo Stein's visit to a small Paris gallery run by art dealer Ambroise Vollard. There, stacked in dusty piles, Stein found a number of paintings by Paul Cézanne, an obscure French artist who would later be recognized as one of the founders of *L'Art Moderne*—modern art. Stein bought a Cézanne landscape, *The Spring House*, the first of many paintings that would make him one of the founding collectors of modern art.

"Life was then cheap in Paris," recalled Leo Stein later. "Rents were low, food was not dear, we had no doctor's bills." He and his sister had enough money, sent to them every month by their brother Michael, to live comfortably and to indulge in such occasional luxuries as books, travel, or paintings.

One day in 1904, Michael Stein, who had recently moved with his wife and son to Paris, told Leo and Gertrude that their investments had made an unexpected profit. This meant that they had a little extra money; not spending it, they decided, would be a "criminal waste." Brother and sister rushed to Vollard's, where, at very low prices, they bought two paintings by Cézanne, two by Paul Gauguin, and two by Jean Renoir—all now recognized as giants of modern art.

In the fall of 1905, all of the Parisian Steins—Gertrude, Leo, Michael, and his wife, Sally—visited the Autumn Salon, an annual exhibition of new art-

French art dealer Ambroise Vollard, portrayed here by Pablo Picasso, was an early supporter of such avant-garde painters as Cézanne, Henri Matisse, and Picasso himself.

A Stein family portrait, made in Paris in 1907, shows (left to right) Leo, Gertrude, an unidentified friend, Sally, and Michael. Standing in the foreground is Sally and Michael's son, Allan.

ists' work. The entire family was stunned by the sight of *Femme au Chapeau* (Woman with the Hat), a remarkable painting by a young artist named Henri Matisse. The picture, a highly unconventional portrait of the artist's wife, was causing an immense scandal in Paris. Traditionalists regarded Matisse's bold, slashing strokes of vivid paint as a bad joke, if not an insult to art itself. "A paint pot has been flung in the face of the public!" shrilled one critic; another called Matisse a "*fauve*," or wild animal.

The Steins, seldom part of any mainstream, thought *Femme au Chapeau* was wonderful. "This picture by Matisse," wrote Gertrude Stein later, "seemed perfectly natural"; she "could not understand why it infuriated everybody." After a family conference, Leo and Gertrude Stein decided to buy it. They paid 450 francs (about $90), a fortune to the impoverished Matisse and his family. After the sale, Matisse's fortunes began to rise. All the Steins, including Michael and Sally, kept on buying his paintings; within a few years his work was commanding top prices from art dealers and collectors all over Europe.

Matisse became a frequent visitor at 27 rue de Fleurus, and as Gertrude Stein later noted, he "brought people,

everybody brought somebody, and they came at any time and it began to be a nuisance, and it was in this way that Saturday evenings began." Stein's Saturday "evenings" were soon an important part of life for the cultural elite of Paris, who came to talk, to listen, to look at the Steins' growing collection of modern art, and to see the Steins themselves. Even in their own artistic

Paul Gauguin painted this canvas, Faa-Iheihe, *while he was living in Tahiti in the 1890s. In 1904 Gertrude and Leo Stein bought* Sunflowers *and* Three Tahitians, *also created by Gauguin during his stay on the Pacific island.*

Surrounded by paintings he and his sister have collected, Leo Stein enjoys a quiet moment in the studio at 27 rue de Fleurus.

circle, Gertrude and Leo Stein were unusual; they laughed loudly at whatever amused them, smoked cigars, and liked to wear brown corduroy robes with sandals and wool socks.

The "evenings" were gala, unpredictable affairs. The Steins' callers included the cream of Paris's creative people: poets, painters, sculptors, singers, dancers, comedians, art critics, and writers. They told each other's fortunes, read from their latest works, sang, danced, argued long into the night about the latest art exhibits and musical compositions. One poet, according to an observer, would often "dance barefooted, or improvise plays in which he was always the main actor." Another would recite his latest poems: "Oh how badly he spoke his own verse, and how he loved to recite it!" recalled the witness, "although he managed to move us nonetheless."

Often present at the "evenings" were the Steins' friends from Baltimore, Claribel and Etta Cone. The sisters, who

Stein, at the age of 36, relaxes with some of her favorite companions—the paintings and sculpture with which she and her brother filled their Paris apartment.

Matisse's Femme au Chapeau (Woman with the Hat), *now considered a masterpiece, infuriated most Parisians when it was first exhibited in 1905. Gertrude and Leo Stein bought it for $90.*

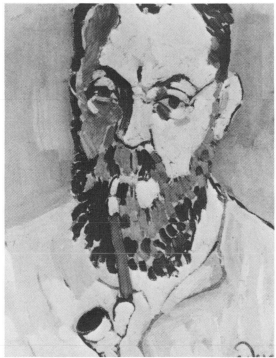

Matisse, smoking a pipe in this portrait by André Derain, was poor and unknown when the Steins bought one of his paintings in 1905. A few years later, he was wealthy and famous.

had inherited a fortune, were eager to buy paintings; the Steins were delighted to introduce the wealthy women to their needy artist friends. Like Gertrude Stein, Etta Cone was an enthusiastic shopper, and the two women spent many afternoons strolling the fashionable streets of Paris and browsing in elegant stores.

Etta Cone also made herself extremely useful to Stein by typing her manuscripts. Stein, who usually worked at night in order to escape interruption, composed all her manuscripts in large, bold, but almost unreadable handwriting. Cone spent hours patiently deciphering her friend's scrawls; the first Stein work to emerge from her typewriter would be *Three Lives*.

Another favored guest at 27 rue de Fleurus was Spanish artist Pablo Picasso. The Steins had become acquainted with him in 1905, after Leo had bought a Picasso painting, *Jeune Fille aux Fleurs* (Girl with Flowers).

When Leo Stein bought Picasso's Jeune Fille aux Fleurs (Girl with Flowers), *Gertrude Stein was furious. Her brother soon abandoned Picasso, but she became the painter's good friend and ardent supporter.*

According to Leo Stein's memoirs, his sister had voted against the picture, but he had bought it, anyway. When he brought it home, Gertrude, who was eating, slammed down her fork. "Now you've spoiled my appetite," she said. "I hated that picture with the feet like a monkey's."

The artist who had painted the "monkey feet," however, was another matter. When Picasso called at the rue de Fleurus apartment, Stein was utterly charmed. He reminded her, she wrote later, of "a good-looking bootblack. He was thin dark, alive with big pools of eyes and a violent but not rough way." She recalled the first time he came to dinner. When she absent-mindedly picked up some bread that was lying near his plate, he grabbed it out of her hand. "This piece of bread is mine!" he shouted. "She laughed," wrote Stein, "and he looked sheepish. That was the beginning of their intimacy." That intimacy, a close friendship punctuated by both fierce quarrels and long, satisfying conversations, would endure for the next 41 years.

Picasso was only 24 years old when he first met Stein. He would eventually be recognized as one of the 20th century's greatest artists, but in 1905 he was both poor and virtually unknown. He would never forget the enthusiastic support he received from Stein and her brother. They bought dozens of his paintings, frequently fed and enter-

Picasso was only 24 years old when he met Gertrude Stein in 1905. She liked him immediately, delighted by what she called his "violent but not rough way."

tained him, and brought his work to the attention of their friends, including the free-spending Cone sisters.

When Etta Cone, a frequent visitor to Picasso's studio, expressed interest in the artist's discarded sketches, Stein encouraged her to buy them for two dollars each—a sum both Stein and Picasso thought absurdly high. Eventually, the many Picasso sketches and paintings acquired by Etta and Claribel Cone would form the core of the Bal-

timore Museum of Art's important Cone Collection.

In 1905, Picasso asked Stein to pose for a portrait. She was flattered; this would be the first time in eight years that Picasso had used a model.

Art scholars divide Picasso's work into "periods," each representing a new way of seeing and interpreting the world. In his earliest creative years, between 1901 and 1904—his "blue period"—most of his paintings evoke a mood of melancholy, of sorrow for the lonely and dispossesed of the world. In his "rose period," 1905 to 1906, he abandoned the blue shades that had characterized his earlier work, painting instead in pinks, grays, and occasional flashes of brighter colors. By the time he met and painted Stein, he was also experimenting with primitivism. He produced powerful and highly expressive portraits in this style, his subjects' faces and figures often resembling carved masks.

Picasso's painting of Stein, which is considered one of his masterpieces, emerged after some 90 posing sessions. It shows her seated, wearing her favorite brown corduroy dress and coral brooch. She appears monumental, brooding, her mouth straight, her eyes prominent, her nose angular.

When the likeness was completed in the spring of 1906, Picasso gave it to Stein, who was delighted. "I was and I still am satisfied with my portrait," she wrote later, "for me, it is I, and it is the

Picasso's portrait of Stein, which now hangs in New York City's Metropolitan Museum of Art, pleased its subject. "For me," she said, "it is I."

only reproduction of me which is always I, for me." Other people, including Leo, however, disliked it; Stein, they said, did not resemble the painting. Told of their remarks, Picasso just smiled. "She will," he said.

The artist now began to experiment with yet another style, this one both truly revolutionary and highly controversial. Cubism, as the new mode was called, presented the world in an entirely new way. Instead of showing objects as they appear to the human eye, Picasso and the other Cubists broke the subjects of their paintings into abstract, cubelike forms.

By reducing natural forms to their geometric equivalents, the Cubists hoped to discover their "reality." Traditional painters showed their subjects from one angle only, much as a camera does. Cubists, on the other hand, showed their subjects as a whole, as though they could be seen from all sides at the same time. Some of Picasso's paintings of people, for example, show both eyes as well as the profile of the face.

Picasso's Cubism had much in common with Stein's approach to writing; both aimed at presenting the essence of their subjects rather than their obvious photographic likenesses. Both artists, furthermore, took daring steps into uncharted terrain. Unsurprisingly, Stein was attracted to Picasso's new style. "There are two geniuses in art today," she told him, "you in painting and I in literature." Leo Stein, however, disagreed. Along with a number of Picasso's other early admirers, he was both baffled and annoyed by the artist's new style. He called Picasso's first major Cubist painting, *Les Demoiselles d'Avignon*, "incoherent" and a "horrible mess." Leo later noted that when "somebody asked me whether I didn't think [Picasso's later work] mad, I said sadly, 'No, it isn't as interesting as that; it's only stupid.' "

Picasso's Les Demoiselles d'Avignon, *which sparked the Cubist movement, is now regarded as a pivotal work in the history of modern art. In 1907 Leo Stein called it a "horrible mess."*

All her life, Stein had followed in her brother's footsteps; now she began to question his leadership. The siblings' strong difference of opinion about Picasso and the Cubists signaled the beginning of a rift between them. Leo, Stein later wrote, "continued to believe in what he was saying when he was arguing, and I began not to find it interesting."

Soon after Stein began to loosen her ties to her brother, she formed a new relationship, one that was to prove both more rewarding and more permanent. In 1907, she met Alice B. Toklas.

Swiss artist Felix Vallotton saw Gertrude Stein as a massive, somber figure. His 1907 portrait shows her in the brown corduroy robe and blue necklace that she usually wore at her "evenings."

FIVE

The End of the "Old Life"

In 1907, Gertrude Stein was 33 years old. She had completed two books, been painted by Pablo Picasso, and become a central figure in the artistic circles of Paris. She was, however, no closer to achieving *la gloire* than she had been when she left medical school six years earlier. She had yet to find a publisher interested in her books; to her distress, not even her brother Leo seemed to think much of them.

Upon finishing *Three Lives* in 1905, Stein had shown the manuscript to Leo and to her sister-in-law. Sally Stein had been enthusiastic, but Leo Stein had been uncharacteristically silent, which depressed her. "I am afraid," she wrote to a friend, "that I can never write the great American novel."

In *The Making of Americans*, she commented indirectly on her brother's chilly reaction to her work. "Disillusionment in living," she wrote, "is the finding out nobody agrees with you not [even] those that are fighting for you. . . . Then you say you will write for yourself and strangers, you will be for yourself and strangers and then this makes an old man or an old woman of you."

In addition to the strain caused by their literary disagreements, the tension caused by their differing assessments of Picasso's work continued to weaken their relationship. Stein had always considered her brother brilliant, but his negative attitudes had undermined her faith in him. She was ready to form stronger attachments to others.

In the fall of 1907, Sally Stein invited her sister-in-law to meet a visitor from San Francisco, 28-year-old Alice B.

The picturesque buildings, gaslit streets, and low rents of Paris's Rive Gauche (Left Bank), *the site of the Steins' apartment, attracted many artists and writers.*

Toklas. The meeting was to be a turning point in the lives of both Stein and Toklas.

Toklas later recalled her first reaction to Stein, who had just returned from a trip to Tuscany, Italy: "She was a golden brown presence, burned by the Tuscan sun and with a golden glint in her warm brown hair. She was dressed in a warm brown corduroy suit.... Her voice.... was unlike any one else's voice—deep, full, velvety, like a great contralto's, like two voices.

She was large and heavy with delicate small hands and a beautifully modelled and unique head."

Stein and her circle were, in turn, impressed by Toklas. One member of the group described her as "slight and dark, with beautiful gray eyes hung with black lashes—and she had a drooping, Jewish nose, and her eyelids drooped, and the corners of her red mouth and the lobes of her ears drooped under the black folded Hebraic hair, weighted down, as they were, with long heavy Oriental earrings." Toklas, added this observer, "looked like Leah, out of the Old Testament, in her half-Oriental getup."

When she attended one of Stein's famous "evenings," Toklas—who had spent her adult years quietly keeping house for her father—was astonished. Here was a crowd of noisy, uninhibited artists, people who valued creativity and self-expression far more than conventional manners and morals, people utterly unlike the sedate middle-class citizens among whom she had been raised. And here were walls covered with exuberant modern art, which was not at all like the staid, traditional paintings in the houses of her San Francisco acquaintances.

She was uneasy about the art she saw at 27 rue de Fleurus. "The pictures were so strange," she wrote later, "that one quite instinctively looked at anything rather than at them just at first." She was, however, intrigued by the pictures' creators, particularly Pablo Picasso and his "marvelous, all-seeing brilliant black eyes." She also admired his wit, laughing loudly at his remark about the many Americans who gathered at Stein's apartment: *Ils sont pas des hommes, ils sont pas des femmes*" he said, "*ils sont des Américains.*" (*"They are not men, they are not women, they are Americans."*)

Stein and Toklas were comfortable with each other from the start. Stein arranged French lessons for the

Picasso, seen here in a self-portrait, was a source of rancor between the Steins. Gertrude called Picasso's paintings the work of a "genius"; Leo called them an "utter abomination."

younger woman, took her to concerts and galleries, and introduced her to the young artists of Paris. Eager to help her new friend in her work, Toklas took on the formidable job of typing the huge manuscript for *The Making of Americans*, the book Stein had been working on for several years. She also started correcting the printer's proofs of *Three Lives*, for which Stein had at last arranged publication.

Getting *Three Lives* into print had been a long, hard job. One American publisher had rejected it as "too unconventional" and "too literary." Another, conceding that it had "a certain originality" and "sincere simplicity," turned it down because its "strain of intensity was too unbroken" and its portraits "too infinitesimally detailed." Finally, a literary agent friend had suggested that Stein pay for the book's publication herself; she agreed, signing a contract with New York City's Grafton Press in 1908.

After he read *Three Lives*, the president of Grafton Press wrote to Stein. He told her that the manuscript had "some pretty bad slips in grammar, probably caused in the typewriting," and suggested a number of corrections. Outraged, Stein instructed him to change nothing. The publisher bowed to his client's wishes, but not without a parting shot. "I want to say frankly," he wrote her, "that I think you have written a very peculiar book and it will be a hard thing to make people take it seriously."

Three Lives arrived in American bookstores in 1910. Some critics recognized its importance; the distinguished scholar Carl Van Doren called it "the beginning of American literature," and the *Kansas City Star* said it was "remarkable," "subtle," and "a very masterpiece of realism." On the whole, however, Stein was disappointed by the book's reception in her native land. Few people read it, and most of those who did were critical; it not only dealt with "unpleasant things," they said; it was "dreadfully immoral." Six months after publication, only 73 of the 500 copies printed had been sold.

Not even Stein's mentor and admirer William James was encouraging. He wrote her a letter explaining that he had lost the copy she had sent him. "You see what a swine I am to have pearls cast before him!" he said, adding, "I promise you that it shall be read *some* time!" Stein was never to learn what her old friend thought of the book; three months later, the Paris

Leo Stein served as a model for this 1906 Picasso portrait. Like much of the painter's early work, it is now part of the Cone Collection at the Baltimore Museum of Art.

newspaper *Le Figaro* reported the loss of "one of the greatest philosophical minds of the age." William James was dead at the age of 68.

Some critics questioned Stein's competence to write about black characters, but "Melanctha," the longest story in *Three Lives*, was praised by many black readers. James Weldon Johnson, author of *The Autobiography of an Ex-Colored Man*, called Stein "the first . . . white writer to write a story of love between a Negro man and woman and deal with them as normal members of the human family." Novelist Nella Larsen, who wrote *Passing*, composed a letter to Stein in which she said, "I never cease to wonder. . . . why you and not some one of us should so accurately have caught the spirit of this race of mine."

Many years after its publication, Richard Wright, the eminent author of *Native Son*, read *Three Lives*. He said that "Melanctha" had filled him with "delight" but that he wanted to see how other blacks reacted to it. "I gathered a group of semi-literate Negro stockyard workers into a Black Belt [Deep South] basement and read 'Melanctha' aloud to them," he wrote. "They understood every word. Enthralled, they slapped their thighs, howled, laughed, stomped, and interrupted me constantly to comment upon the characters."

After the publication of *Three Lives*, Stein continued to work on *The Making of Americans*, which she was not to complete until 1911 and which was not to be published until 1925. Stein's handwriting, never clear, had become increasingly difficult to decipher; sometimes she could not read it herself. Alice Toklas, however, made it her business to learn to translate her friend's scrawl. Stein wrote at night—sometimes all night. Toklas got up early each day to begin her work while Stein slept. She thoroughly enjoyed the job, later referring to this period as

Picasso takes a break with a friend. Always fond of animals, the artist shared his studio with a menagerie that included numerous stray dogs and cats, a white mouse, and a monkey.

Alice B. Toklas (left) and Stein relax at 27 rue de Fleurus. At Stein's right is Cézanne's portrait of his wife; on the wall behind her is Picasso's The Architect's Table.

"a very happy time." She said it "was like living history" and remembered that she had "hoped it would go on forever."

Toklas did more than transcribe Stein's work. She acted as a sounding board for the writer's ideas, often contributing impressions of her own that wound up in the manuscript. Stein was a tireless walker; as she and Toklas tramped through the streets of Paris or hiked in the woods outside the city, they talked constantly, usually about the characters in *The Making of Americans*.

As well as filling the roles of Stein's secretary, literary consultant, and cherished companion, Toklas acted as her cook on the housekeeper's days off. Always a hearty eater, Stein missed American food; Toklas obliged by preparing her favorite dishes, one of which was roast turkey stuffed with mushrooms, chestnuts, and oysters.

American novelist Richard Wright, long an admirer of Stein, finally met her in 1946. She persuaded him to settle in Paris, where he remained until his death in 1960.

Famed for its Roman, medieval, and Renaissance monuments, Segovia is crowned by a 16th-century Gothic cathedral. The ancient Spanish city was one of the stops on the 1912 trip Toklas and Stein took through Spain.

More and more, the relationship of the two women came to resemble a marriage. Like many couples, they invented special names for one another: Stein called Toklas "Pussy"; to Toklas, Stein was "Lovey."

Stein had spent a brief but pleasant vacation with her brother in Spain in 1901; in 1912 she decided to revisit that country, this time with Toklas. Setting out in May, the two spent the summer observing religious processions, attending Catholic services in city cathedrals and country churches, and watching Spanish dancers in music halls and cafés. They also visited the Prado, Madrid's great museum of art, where they studied the paintings of Spanish artists Francisco Goya, El Greco, and Diego Velázquez.

In Madrid, Spain's capital, Stein insisted on taking Toklas to the bullfights. The often brutal spectacle was not at all to Toklas's taste, but with her companion's help, she managed to sit through several events. When a man or a horse was injured, Stein would tell Toklas to close her eyes; after the wounded had been dragged from the ring, she would allow her to open them again.

The two American women attracted attention wherever they went. Despite the broiling sun, Stein wore her standard heavy corduroy dresses. She completed her outfit with a straw hat, sandals with long, pointed toes, and an amber-headed cane. Toklas, who had adopted what she called her "Spanish disguise"—a long black silk dress, black gloves, a black fan, and a large black hat adorned with brightly colored artificial flowers—reminded one observer of "a nun on a spree." Assuming that the travelers were eccentric noblewomen, or even religious officials, Spaniards treated them with awed respect.

In a letter to a friend, Stein wrote, "As we travel, me in my usual brown garb, many peasants have mistaken me for a high church authority. Once when I was taking a walk, a group followed me and when I sat down they wanted to kiss my ring, thinking I was a bishop whom they were expecting to arrive in the town. I love the attention. Alice thinks I'm sacrilegious."

Throughout the journey, Stein kept writing, filling notebook after notebook with "word portraits" of the people and places she saw. These short experimental pieces, which were collected and published two years later in a book called *Tender Buttons*, were the most abstract and difficult works she had produced so far. One example, inspired by a diamond-bedecked singer in Madrid:

Not so dots large dressed dots, big sizes, less laced, less laced diamonds, diamonds white, diamonds bright, diamonds in the in the light, diamonds light diamonds door diamonds hanging to be four, two four, all before, this bean, lessly, all most, a best, willow, vest, a green guest, guest, go go go go go go, go. Go go. Not guessed. Go go.

Toasted susie is my ice-cream.

Another piece in *Tender Buttons*, "This Is This Dress, Aider," consists of 32 words:

Aider, why aider why whow, whow stop touch, aider whow, aider stop the muncher, muncher munchers.

A jack in kill her, a jack in, makes a meadowed king, makes a to let.

Even shorter is the prose poem entitled "Dining":

Dining is west.

Written in Spain, homeland of Pablo Picasso, *Tender Buttons* can be seen as a verbal version of that artist's Cubism. Stein herself confirmed the similarity; talking to a friend soon after the Spanish trip, she said, "Well, Pablo is doing abstract portraits in painting. I am trying to do abstract portraits in *my* medium, *words*."

Continuing to write furiously when she returned to Paris, Stein also continued her efforts to get published. *Camera Work*, a New York magazine, ran the "portraits" she wrote of Matisse and Picasso, but most publishers rejected her work as "too difficult."

A classic response came in 1912 from a British publisher, who returned a manuscript with a letter parodying her own style. "Dear Madam," it said, "I am only one, only one, only one.... Being only one, having only one pair of eyes, having only one time, having only one life, I cannot read your manuscript three or four times. Not even one time.... Hardly one copy would sell here. Hardly one. Hardly one."

Although she was having trouble finding a publisher, Stein was nonetheless becoming a literary celebrity. Her new fame was due in part to a word portrait she had written about a friend named Mabel Dodge, a wealthy, much-married American socialite and art collector. In 1912, after Stein and Toklas had spent a few weeks with Dodge at her luxurious villa in Florence, Stein wrote a piece called "Portrait of Mabel Dodge at the Villa Curonia." Containing such sentences as "The intention is what if application has that accident results are reappearing," the "Portrait" was not easy to understand. But it delighted Dodge, who immediately paid for its publication, creating a buzz of interest among her wide circle of rich and influential friends.

Soon after the appearance of the "Portrait," a group of New Yorkers be-

A Spanish matador narrowly escapes a charging bull. Stein enjoyed bullfights, but Toklas found them horrifying; she covered her eyes during most of the action.

gan to organize a huge exhibition of modern art in New York City. Among the collectors asked to lend paintings to the show were Leo and Gertrude Stein, who obliged with a Matisse and two Picassos.

The 1913 exhibit, known as the Armory Show, commanded worldwide interest. Publicized by countless newspaper and magazine stories, it became the focus of conversation in fashionable salons from New York to London to Paris. As a contributor to the show and author of the now famous Mabel Dodge "Portrait," Stein was also in the news. "You are just on the eve of *bursting*!" wrote Dodge to Stein before the show opened. "Everybody wherever I go.... is talking of Gertrude Stein!"

The Armory Show, which was attended by almost a million people, was a sensation. The public came to praise, to jeer, and to gape in astonishment at revolutionary paintings and sculptures by such artists as Pablo Picasso, Henri Matisse, Paul Cézanne, Vincent van Gogh, Paul Gauguin, Georges Braque, Fernand Léger, and Wassily Kandinsky. The most controversial work in the show was Marcel Duchamp's surrealistic *Nude Descending a Staircase*, a haunting but puzzling canvas that one irritated critic compared to "an explosion in a shingle factory."

Amid the torrents of newsprint about the show were a number of articles about Stein. One of them said

Wealthy art collector Mabel Dodge, thrilled to be the subject of a Stein "word portrait," published it in 1912. The ensuing publicity helped make Stein's name a household word in the United States.

that although she had been accused of using the English language "roughly, uncouthly, and brutally, or madly, stupidly, and hideously," Stein's writing was "so exquisitely rhythmical and cadenced that if we read it aloud and receive it as pure sound, it is like a kind of sensuous music."

Stein was gossiped about in drawing rooms and galleries, discussed in lecture halls and scholarly publications, and made the butt of newspapers' jokes. The *Chicago Tribune*, reacting to the outrage some conservatives had

Parked outside Manhattan's 69th Regiment Armory in 1913, limousines await their owners. Inside, thousands of people gaped at the Armory Show, a watershed in modern art history.

expressed over the Matisse *Blue Nude*, which Stein had lent to the Armory Show, published a "poem" about it:

I called the canvas *Cow with Cud*
And hung it on the line,
Altho' to me 'twas vague as mud,
'Twas clear to Gertrude Stein.

Perhaps as a result of all this publicity, Stein was finally offered a publishing contract. In 1914, an avant-garde New York City publisher interested in printing experimental literature, Claire Marie Press, announced its wish to print *Tender Buttons*, guaranteeing Stein a royalty of 10 percent on the first 500 copies sold and 15 percent on all additional copies. This would be the first time she would not have to pay

the printing costs for one of her books. She quickly signed the contract.

Claire Marie Press—its motto was "New Books for Exotic Tastes"—soon released a brochure describing its new author: "She is a ship that flies no flag and she is outside the law of art, but she descends on every port and leaves a memory of her visits."

Tender Buttons, which was divided into three sections, "Objects," "Food," and "Rooms," was greeted by a storm of ridicule and anger. Describing it, critics used such words as "barbaric," "unintelligible," and "stupid." The reviewer for the *Atlantic Monthly* quoted several of Stein's paragraphs, then wrote, "After a hundred lines of this I

The Armory Show would raise few eyebrows today, but in 1913 its entries scandalized viewers. One art critic called the Cubist collection a "chamber of horrors."

wish to scream, I wish to burn the book, I am in agony."

Mocked and criticized or not, Stein had become famous; by the winter of 1914 few artists, writers, or intellectuals considered a trip to Paris complete unless they had called on her at 27 rue de Fleurus. Her increasing celebrity became more and more irritating to her brother Leo, who had already felt jealous of his sister's close relationship with Alice Toklas and resented the rising fame of Pablo Picasso.

In a letter to a friend, Leo Stein said, "As [Gertrude and I] have come to maturity, we find that there is practi-

cally nothing under the heavens that we don't. . . . disagree about." His sister and her friend Picasso, added Stein, "are using their intellects, which they ain't got, to do what would need the finest critical tact, which they ain't got neither, and they are to my belief turning out the most Godalmighty rubbish."

In the spring of 1914, Leo and Gertrude Stein, who had lived together since they shared a house in Baltimore in 1897, decided to part company. They sold some of their paintings and divided up the rest; he kept the Renoirs and Cézannes, and she kept the

This cartoon lampooning the Armory Show was reprinted in hundreds of U.S. newspapers. For many Americans, "The 'New Art' Fest" was the biggest joke of the year.

The Armory Show's star attraction was Nude Descending a Staircase. The work of 26-year-old French artist Marcel Duchamp caused a near riot when it was first displayed.

Picassos. She stayed in the Paris apartment; he took the furniture and moved to Florence. From there, he wrote her a letter, saying, "I hope that we will all live happily ever after and maintain our respective and due proportions while sucking gleefully our respective oranges."

Despite the differences between brother and sister, they had been extremely close, and the parting was not easy for either of them. As a mutual friend later observed, "Gertrude was possessed by a singular devotion to Leo; she admired and loved him in a way a man is seldom admired and loved; it was part of her profound temperament." Stein later remarked sadly, "We always had been together, and now we were never at all together. Little by little we never met again." Then she added a prophetic line: "In the spring and early summer of nineteen fourteen the old life was over."

Vacationing in Venice, Italy, Stein and Toklas feed pigeons. "The pigeon on the grass alas," from Four Saints in Three Acts, *is one of Stein's most-quoted lines.*

SIX

The "Sibyl of Montparnasse"

In the summer of 1914, at the age of 40, Gertrude Stein got some good news: An English publisher, John Lane, had decided to produce a British edition of *Three Lives*. He asked her to come to London to sign a contract, and she happily obliged. On July 6, she and Toklas boarded a steamer and crossed the English Channel. Stein was excited by the prospect of the new edition of her book; perhaps she would find literary *gloire* in the country of Shakespeare and Milton. As it turned out, however, the topic of the day would not be literature.

A week before Stein and Toklas left France, newspapers had carried stories from the city of Sarajevo in Bosnia (a region that would become part of Yugoslavia in 1946), where Archduke Francis Ferdinand of Austria had been shot and killed by a Serbian terrorist. The news seemed unimportant to many people in the West; they did not

see how the murder of an obscure Central European aristocrat could affect them. Well-informed observers, however, were uneasy. Tensions among Europe's powerful nations had been steadily increasing; the whole continent, in fact, had been compared to a powder keg. The assassination of the archduke might prove to be the spark that set it off.

These observers, of course, were correct. A month after the murder in Sarajevo, Austria declared war on Serbia, and czarist Russia lined up its armies at Austria's border. A week later, Germany invaded Belgium and declared war on Russia and France. By early August, the roar of cannon fire across Europe signaled the start of World War I.

Stein and Toklas were among those who considered the early rumors of war exaggerated. They expected to spend three weeks in England, then return to their peaceful existence in Paris. After Stein signed her book contract, which she called a "gratifying climax," on July 31, she and Toklas left London for a long country weekend with friends.

On August 4, England declared war on Germany, joining the side of Russia and France. During the war's first weeks, the German army seemed unstoppable. After smashing through Belgium, it headed west; Paris, it appeared, would soon fall to the onrushing German troops. Stein and Toklas spent the next 11 weeks with their English hosts, unsure about the future and deeply concerned about their friends in Paris, about Stein's manuscripts—the only copies of which were at the apartment at 27 rue de Fleurus—and about Paris itself, the city they both loved.

All England rejoiced over the news that arrived on September 19: After a huge battle on the Marne River, near Paris, the Germans had been stopped; Paris was saved. Stein and Toklas wept when they heard the news. With travel restrictions eased, they returned to Paris, where they found their apartment safe. Paris, however, seemed like a different place. The once-sparkling city was dark and quiet, many of its stores shuttered, most of its able-bodied men gone to the front. In the daytime, the streets were filled with wounded soldiers, tattered refugees, and long lines of people waiting

Archduke Francis Ferdinand of Austria and his wife, Sophie, fall to an assassin's bullets at Sarajevo on June 28, 1914. The murder sparked World War I, history's worst conflict to that date.

for their rations of scarce food and fuel. At night the eerie silence was often shattered by the shriek of air-raid sirens.

Stein packed up her manuscripts, sent them to New York for safekeeping, and prepared to resume her regular life. Many artist friends had left Paris, but Picasso, who had remained, was a frequent guest at the rue de Fleurus. As German airships dropped their bombs on Paris, he and Stein would continue to hold long conversations as though everything were normal. "It was a strange winter," recalled Stein later, "and nothing and everything happened."

In the spring of 1915, a friend invited Stein and Toklas to visit him on the Spanish island of Majorca; they accepted gratefully. There they relaxed in the warm sunshine, ate well, watched bullfights, and followed the war from a distance. Stein read reviews—most of them discouraging—of *Tender Buttons*, which had been published the previous June. Unshaken by their mockery, she continued to write, turning out a growing stack of poems and experimental plays.

Much of the work Stein did during this period was published in 1922 under the title *Geography and Plays*. The volume contains such plays as *Do Let Us Go Away*, *For the Country Entirely*, and *Counting Her Dresses*. Consisting entirely of dialogue and containing no plots, character development, scenery, or action, these plays are early versions of the dramatic style later known as "Theater of the Absurd." The nondramatic pieces from this collection, most of them clearly addressed to Toklas, are, however, among Stein's most easily understood writings. Two examples of these works are:

Alright I will be natural.
B is for birthday baby and blessed,
S is for sweetie sweetie and sweetie.
Y is for you and u is for me and we are as happy as happy can be.

and

And some day we will be rich. You'll see. It won't be a legacy, it won't be selling anything, it won't be purchasing, it will just be irresistible and then we will spend money and buy everything a dog a Ford letter paper, furs, a hat, kinds of purses, and nearly something new that we have not yet been careful about.

Geography and Plays also included "Sacred Emily." In it was the line that would become the best known and most often quoted of all Stein's writing, "Rose is a rose is a rose is a rose."

During their stay on Majorca, Stein and Toklas received letters from friends in France who were working to help the war effort. After a year of Spanish sunshine, the pair decided that they, too, should volunteer their services. They returned to Paris, where one morning they saw a young American woman wearing a military uniform and driving a car emblazoned "American Fund for French Wounded." Inquiring about the organization, they learned its mission was to distribute

Waiting for news bulletins, worried Parisians crowd the city's streets in June 1914. Stein and Toklas, confident that war would be averted, sailed for England in early July.

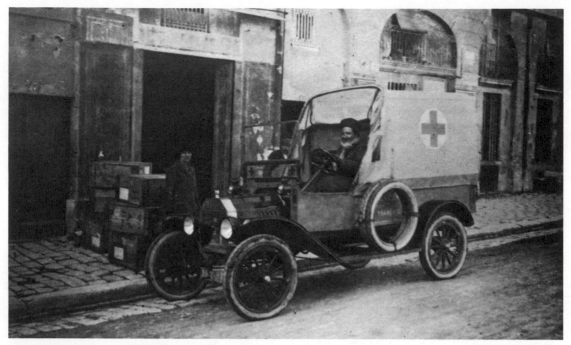

As Toklas watches warily from the sidewalk, Stein guns the motor of "Auntie," the Ford truck she drove during World War I. She loved to drive, but was notorious for her recklessness behind the wheel.

supplies to military hospitals throughout France.

"There, that is what we are going to do," said Toklas to Stein, adding, "You will drive the car and I will do the rest." After learning that they would have to provide their own vehicle, Stein wrote to a wealthy cousin in the United States, asking him to send her a Ford van. While she was waiting for her cousin's contribution to the war effort, she took driving lessons.

She finally learned to operate a car, but as one observer remarked, she "was to display certain pecularities as a driver." One of them was a refusal to

put the car into reverse for any reason. Another was her habit of carrying on animated conversations while driving; this could be unnerving to her passengers, especially when she turned to talk to them in the backseat, her foot firmly planted on the accelerator. She liked to drive as fast as possible, but because she scorned road maps, she would often drive very fast in the wrong direction.

When the car arrived from the United States in the spring of 1917, Stein and Toklas set out for Perpignan, a city in southwestern France that was near several military hospitals. They

Stein (seated, second from right) and Toklas (standing at far left) line up with staff members of the American Fund for French Wounded in 1917.

had named the car "Auntie," after one of Stein's aunts who "always behaved admirably in emergencies and behaved fairly well most times if she was properly flattered." The two women designed their own uniforms: Toklas wore a British officer's jacket and a pith helmet like those worn by British explorers in Africa; Stein wore a huge military overcoat, a Russian cavalryman's hat, and sandals. Together, remarked a painter friend, "they looked extremely strange."

Oddly attired or not, Stein and Toklas were welcome in southern France, where they spent the next year and a half delivering much-needed supplies to the wounded. As they traveled from one hospital to another, they gave lifts to as many soldiers as they could squeeze into "Auntie," and at each hospital they visited the injured men and distributed cigarettes and clothing. In a poem about her war work, Stein wrote:

We meet a great many without suits.
We help them into them.
They need them to read them to feed
them to lead them.
And in their ignorance.
No one is ignorant.
And in their ignorance.
We please them.

Celebrating the conclusion of World War I, Parisians gather at the Place de l'Opéra on November 11, 1918. "It all finally came to an end," wrote Stein, "and peace was upon us."

Sylvia Beach works at her bookshop, Shakespeare & Company, in the 1920s. A close friend of Stein, Beach was besieged by young writers eager to meet the "Sibyl of Montparnasse."

World War I, which claimed more than 10 million lives, finally ended on November 11, 1918. Still, Toklas and Stein's services were needed; thousands of peasants, uprooted by the fighting that had raged through the French countryside, were returning home to ravaged houses and farms. Until the spring of 1919, the two American women worked tirelessly, distributing food and clothing to the dazed refugees. Their work over at last, they returned to Paris. At first they found it, Toklas recalled later, "more beautiful, vital and inextinguishable than ever." They soon realized, however, that its mood had changed.

Paris, observed Stein, had become "a restless and disturbed world," a city whose inhabitants were trying, with little success, to recreate a way of life that was gone forever. Cubism, which had seemed so exciting before the war, had lost its vitality, and no artistic movement of equal intensity had yet taken its place. People still came to the rue de Fleurus, but many members of "the old crowd," the artists and writers who had once flocked to Stein's "evenings," had been killed in the war; others, Matisse among them, had moved to the country.

Personal relationships, too, suffered in the edgy and unsettled atmosphere of postwar Paris. Even Stein's long-standing friendship with Picasso was affected. Quarreling "over nothing at all," they stopped speaking to each other in 1919. When they resumed their warm association a few years later, neither could remember what they had disagreed about, but the break was real and painful at the time. "Everybody," observed Stein sadly, "ceased to be friends."

Meanwhile, Paris was filling up with new faces. The peace conference that officially ended World War I had drawn thousands of delegates, secretaries, reporters, and writers to the city. Many of them, particularly the young Americans, were bitterly disappointed by the outcome of the conference. They had expected the victors to create the blueprint for a new and better world, a place where human dignity would be respected and guarded, where all individuals could expect justice and equality. Instead, the conference delegates had produced a harsh treaty that punished the defeated nations and redrew national boundaries around the world, ignoring the rights of much of the world's population. To many, the treaty seemed almost to guarantee a brutal sequel to the "war to end all wars," as the recent conflict had been called.

Disillusioned by their own country's abandonment of its goals at the peace conference and attracted by the free-wheeling social and intellectual life of Paris, many young Americans remained in the French capital when the conference ended. Most of them wanted to meet Gertrude Stein.

Few of these Americans had read much of Stein's work. Although she had published *Three Lives* in 1909, the word portraits of Picasso and Matisse in *Camera Work* in 1912, and *Tender Buttons* in 1914, none of the three had sold widely. Nevertheless, Stein was a celebrity, made famous by the innumerable parodies of her work in literary magazines and by colorful stories about the glittering circle that assembled at 27 rue de Fleurus.

Stein was known to be a regular patron of Shakespeare & Company, a Paris bookshop that had first impressed her when she discovered two copies of *Tender Buttons* on its shelves. Eager to meet the mysterious and fascinating Stein, young American writers

Sherwood Anderson, author of the best-selling Winesburg, Ohio, *was introduced to Stein by Sylvia Beach in 1921. He said that after reading Stein's work, he "fell in love with words."*

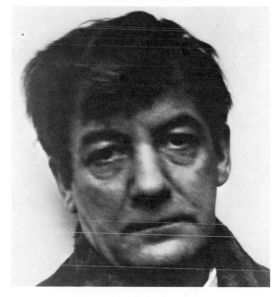

Author Ernest Hemingway conceded that Stein had taught him a great deal about his craft, but he called her a hard task-master. "Writing," he told her, "used to be easy before I met you."

Toklas sits for a 1922 portrait by Man Ray, a young American painter and photographer. His work was publicized by Sylvia Beach, who often displayed it in her shop.

began to haunt the bookshop, which was operated by an American named Sylvia Beach. Stein's admirers, recalled Beach later, "were often 'skeered' to approach her without proper protection. So the poor things would come to me, exactly as if I were a guide from one of the tourist agencies, and beg me to take them to see Gertrude Stein."

In 1921, Beach introduced Stein to Sherwood Anderson, an American novelist who had published the highly successful short-story collection, *Winesburg, Ohio*, in 1919. Some critics had compared Anderson's stories with Stein's "Melanctha" from *Three Lives*, and Anderson himself often credited Stein as his literary mentor. He had told an interviewer that *Tender*

Buttons "excited me as one might grow excited in going into a new and wonderful country where everything is strange."

Stein and Anderson liked each other at once, establishing a friendship that would continue until Anderson's death 20 years later. As well as paying frequent calls on Stein, Anderson sent other writers to the apartment at 27 rue de Fleurus. One of them was a 22-year-old newspaper correspondent named Ernest Hemingway.

An aspiring but as yet unpublished writer of fiction, Hemingway had heard many tales of the "Sibyl of Montparnasse." Stein, who lived in the district of Paris known as Montparnasse, was often referred to as a sibyl, or prophetess. The young American was not disappointed by the apartment on the rue de Fleurus. "It was like one of the best rooms in the finest museum," he wrote later, "except there was a big fireplace and it was warm and comfortable and they gave you good things to eat and tea and natural distilled liqueurs made from purple plums, yellow plums or wild raspberries."

Stein's choice of Toklas as her lifelong mate left no doubt about her sexual preference, but for serious conversation, she preferred to associate with men. The wives of the male writers who visited her were, in fact, not expected to participate in the dialogues at the rue de Fleurus. "They couldn't be kept from coming," noted Sylvia Beach, "but Alice had strict orders to keep them out of the way while Gertrude conversed with the husbands." Stein particularly enjoyed the company of men she considered attractive. Hemingway, noted the 48-year-old Stein, was "extraordinarily good-looking," with "passionately interested" eyes.

Pleased by the young man's obvious respect and affection, Stein began to read his work and to offer advice. She wanted, however, to help Hemingway, not flatter him. When he showed her the draft of his first novel, she said, "There is a great deal of description in this, and not particularly good description. Begin over again and concentrate." In addition, she scolded him for writing explicit sex scenes. "There is no point in it," she said. "It's wrong and it's silly."

Although she sometimes criticized him sternly, Stein genuinely admired Hemingway. She urged him to give up journalism and devote his time and talent to writing fiction. It was she who helped him develop the straightforward, deceptively simple style that was to become his trademark. In a letter to her written after he had published his first book, *Three Stories and Ten Poems*, he said, "But isn't writing a hard job, though? It used to be easy before I met you. I certainly was bad, gosh, I'm awfully bad now but it's a different kind of bad."

Author F. Scott Fitzgerald joins his wife, Zelda, and their daughter, Scottie, for a publisher's publicity shot. Stein awed Fitzgerald; he said her praise "honestly makes me shiver."

Poet Ezra Pound often visited Stein, but he was not among her favorite people. She finally refused to receive him; whenever he proposed to call, she said she would be busy "picking wildflowers."

Hemingway got a chance to repay Stein's kindness in 1923, when he became an assistant editor at *The Transatlantic Review*. He persuaded the publisher of the highly regarded literary magazine to serialize Stein's enormous novel *The Making of Americans*. Stein received the news with delight. Segments of the book began to appear in 1924, but after nine installments, the magazine failed, and publication was discontinued.

Stein's disappointment about the incomplete publication of *The Making of Americans* was eased when another friend of Hemingway's, Robert McAlmon, agreed to publish it in 1925. Almost 1,000 pages long, the book confused readers from its opening page, which begins: "Once an angry man dragged his father along the ground through his own orchard. 'Stop!' cried the groaning old man at last, 'Stop! I did not drag my father beyond this tree.'" The novel, which Stein considered her masterpiece, is subtitled "Being a History of a Family's Progress." Loosely based on various branches of the author's own family, it combines psychology, philosophy, case histories, and observations about life, death, sex, and religion, all tied together by a vague, slow-moving plot.

The reviews of *The Making of Americans* were not kind. The critic for the *Saturday Review of Literature* said it sounded like "conversations in the Tower of Babel"; the *New Republic* said its strongest point was its ability to cause readers "simply to fall asleep"; the *Irish Statesman* said "it must be among the seven longest books in the world." A year after publication, the book had sold 103 copies.

Stein oversees sculptor Jo Davidson as he works on his portrait of her. The two talked constantly during the sitting; Davidson later called the conversation "rich and furious."

Meanwhile, Stein continued to receive the best and the brightest of America's and England's writers at the rue de Fleurus. Soon after *The Making of Americans* appeared, Hemingway brought his friend F. Scott Fitzgerald to Stein's home. Stein was already an admirer of the 29-year-old American novelist, whose *This Side of Paradise* had created a literary sensation five years earlier. She had been particularly impressed with his latest book, *The* predicted that his work would still be read "when many of his well-known contemporaries are forgotten."

The admiration was mutual. Fitzgerald, who had been deeply impressed with *The Making of Americans*, wrote Stein a letter after their first meeting. "My wife and I," he said, "think you a very handsome, very gallant, very kind lady and thought so as soon as we saw you." When Fitzgerald was about to turn 30, he told Stein he was worried about reaching "the end of his youth." The 52-year-old writer assured him that his best work lay ahead of him and said he should write a "great" book, even drawing a line on a piece of paper to show him how thick it should be. Eight years later, Fitzgerald sent her a copy of his major novel, *Tender Is the Night*. Inside the cover, he wrote, "Is this the book you asked for?"

Stein sometimes complained that the young writers in Paris were wasting their lives, drinking and carousing when they should have been at their desks. "You are all a lost generation," she once said. Nevertheless, she reveled in their almost worshipful attention. She did not, however, always enjoy receiving visits from such established literary figures as British poet T. S. Eliot, whose works included *The Waste Land*, and American poet Ezra Pound, best known for his *Cantos*.

She found Eliot's extremely formal British manners stuffy and Pound's nonstop conversation tiring. In *The*

Seated beneath her portrait by Picasso, Stein models the cropped hairstyle she adopted in 1926. Picasso, who thought she should continue to resemble his picture, was not pleased with the new look.

Great Gatsby, which had just been published. Fitzgerald, said Stein, was "the only one of the younger writers who wrote naturally in sentences"; she

Autobiography of Alice B. Toklas, she wrote, "Gertrude Stein liked [Pound] but did not find him amusing. She said he was a village explainer, excellent if you were a village, but if you were not, not."

Among Stein's favorite callers were sculptors Jo Davidson and Jacques Lipchitz, both of whom did portrait sculptures of her. In Lipchitz's likeness, she looks almost Oriental, like a figure of Buddha; in Davidson's, she appears massive, like a farm laborer. She liked both pieces, although she told Davidson that his made her look like "the goddess of pregnancy."

In the new hairstyle she adopted in late 1926, Stein did not look like a "goddess" of anything. Admiring the fashionable "bob" a friend had just gotten, Stein decided to cut her own hair, which she had been wearing in tight braids across her head. Toklas obligingly picked up her scissors and went to work. As her hair got shorter and shorter, Stein liked it better and better, winding up with what is now called a crew cut. Just as Toklas finished her work, Sherwood Anderson appeared on the doorstep. Stein asked him what he thought of the new haircut. Anderson peered at his friend, then smiled. "You look like a monk," he said. Stein was delighted. She would "look like a monk" for the rest of her days.

At the age of 60, Gertrude Stein was at the height of her powers. Energetic and optimistic, she thoroughly enjoyed "la gloire" when she finally achieved it.

SEVEN

La Gloire

By the end of the 1920s, Stein's name and face were familiar to millions of Americans and Europeans. She had been quoted, parodied, photographed, and talked about for decades—but only a few people had read any of her books. She was genuinely puzzled by her lack of popular acceptance and by the common perception that her work was too difficult for most readers. "All this foolishness about my writing being mystic or impressionistic is so stupid," she told an interviewer in 1930. "I write as pure, straight, grammatical English as anyone, more accurate, grammatically, than most. There isn't a single one of my sentences that a schoolchild couldn't diagram."

As she grew older, Stein became more concerned about her legacy. She had been born into the Jewish faith, but she had never practiced any religion. She did not believe in life after death—"When a Jew dies," she always insisted, "he's dead"—but she very much wanted to leave her mark on earth. "I am working for what will endure," she said. Still, she yearned for recognition, for readers, for *la gloire*. In 1933, when she was 59 years old, she got it.

Publishers had long shown their reluctance to take on the books Stein sent them. "You could not find a handful even of careful readers who would think that it was a serious effort," said a typical rejection letter. Many publishers, however, had urged her to write her autobiography. A book about her experiences and her circle of dazzlingly gifted friends, they said, would be sure to sell. Stein's friends, too, had often tried to persuade her to write her memoirs, but she had always refused. "Not possibly" was her standard response to such suggestions.

If anyone were to write a book about her, Stein maintained, it should be

Toklas and Stein take a spin in "Godiva," the successor to "Auntie." When Toklas noted that the car was "nude" (it had no clock or ashtray) Stein had promptly named it after the naked horsewoman of folklore.

Alice Toklas. Teasingly, she suggested that *My Life with the Great* or *Wives of Geniuses I Have Sat With* might be good titles. Joke or no joke, Toklas was not interested. According to Stein, she said later, "I am a pretty good housekeeper and a pretty good gardener and a pretty good needlewoman and a pretty good secretary and a pretty good vet for dogs and I have to do them all at once and I found it difficult to add being a pretty good author."

Clearly, if Stein was going to get a book published, it would have to be an autobiography. And, just as clearly, if anyone was going to write that book, it would have to be Gertrude Stein. Finally, she decided to do it. She would write it, she said, "as simply as Defoe did the autobiography of Robinson Crusoe." By this she meant that although the book would be by and about herself, it would appear to be by and about someone else.

Stein wrote *The Autobiography of Alice B. Toklas* as though she *were* Toklas, using a clear, flowing style that gave readers no problems. She presented not only the stories of her own and Toklas's lives but the history of an era. Here were 25 years of Paris, crowded with such celebrated artists and writers as Pablo Picasso, Henri Matisse, Sherwood Anderson, Ernest Hemingway, F. Scott Fitzgerald, T. S. Eliot, Jo Davidson, and Ezra Pound. Here, too, was a gallery of less famous but equally fascinating people whose paths had crossed Stein's during the last quarter of a century.

The book was a record of artistic and literary movements, a tale of feuds and love affairs, and a rich store of humor, opinion, and gossip, all centered in one of the world's most intriguing cities during one of its most exciting periods. It promised to be a stupendous best-seller.

Stein sent the *Autobiography* manuscript to her New York literary agent, who responded with a cable: "Wild horses couldn't keep me from reading it at once!" He quickly sold the book to New York publisher Harcourt, Brace and arranged for its serialization in the prestigious literary magazine The *Atlantic Monthly*.

Stein had often submitted her work to the *Atlantic*, but its editor, Ellery Sedgwick, had always turned it down. Not even his highly educated readers, he said, would be able to make sense of it. But after he had read the *Autobiography* in early 1933, he fired off an excited letter. "What a delightful book it is," he wrote, "and how glad I am to publish four installments of it! During our long correspondence, I think you felt my constant hope that the time would come when the real Miss Stein would pierce the smoke-screen with which she has always so mischievously surrounded herself.... Hail Gertrude Stein about to arrive!"

Published in September 1933, *The Autobiography of Alice B. Toklas* was an instant success. The critics loved it, and the public snatched up copies as soon as they became available. The first printing sold out even before the official publication date. The result for Stein was immediate stardom and wealth. The sudden inflow of money startled and delighted Stein; although she had never been poor, she had never before earned money on her own.

She made no secret of her pleasure. "I love being rich," she said, "it makes me all cheery inside." She immediately bought a new Ford car for herself and Toklas and an elegant leather coat for

their poodle, Basket. "There is no doubt about it," she wrote later, "there is no pleasure like it, the sudden splendid spending of money and we spent it." When a French translation of the *Autobiography* appeared in 1934, Stein became the toast of Paris. "Everybody

Stein and Picasso, who often quarreled, enjoy a peaceful moment in the 1930s. Encountering Stein after one disagreement, Picasso had slapped her on the shoulder and said, "Oh hell, let's be friends." She turned and kissed him.

invited me to meet somebody, and I went," she wrote later. "It was pleasant being a lion."

Not everybody, however, was pleased with the *Autobiography*. A number of people, including Matisse— whose wife Stein had compared to a horse—raised objections to the accuracy of Stein's recollections and the relevance of her conclusions about art. Questioned by a reporter about the reference to Madame Matisse, Stein insisted she had been misunderstood. "I'm crazy about horses," she said innocently. "You know there are many beautiful horses."

Ernest Hemingway was particularly angry about the book. His once-warm relationship with Stein had cooled rapidly after he had written a cruel parody of her dear friend Sherwood Anderson's work, and the two had seen little of each other in recent years. Now, in the *Autobiography*, Stein called Hemingway, who prided himself on his strength and courage, both "fragile" and "yellow." He sent her a copy of his new book *Death in the Afternoon*, with an inscription inside the cover. It read: "A Bitch Is A Bitch Is A Bitch Is A Bitch. From her pal Ernest Hemingway."

Most outraged of all was Leo Stein, whom the book referred to only as "Gertrude Stein's brother." Refusing even to communicate with his sister, Stein wrote a series of furious letters to friends. "God what a liar she is!" he said, adding, "One of her radical com-

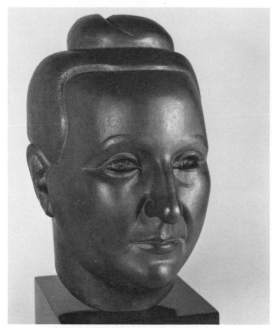

This Buddha-like head of Stein was the work of sculptor Jacques Lipchitz, one of the many artists who appeared in Stein's best-selling book, The Autobiography of Alice B. Toklas.

plexes. . . . made it necessary practically to eliminate me." He called the book a mixture of "rather clever anecdote, stupid brag, and general bosh." He and his sister, he said, were opposites: "She's basically stupid and I'm basically intelligent." Leo and Gertrude Stein never spoke to each other again.

After Stein had gotten used to her newfound popularity and wealth, she began to worry about the effects of success on her work and on her personality. "The moment you or anybody else knows who you are," she wrote, "you are not it, you are what you or

British poet T. S. Eliot, another "character" in the Autobiography, *had also been the subject of one of Stein's word portraits, "A Description of the Fifteenth of November."*

start again, beginning her first—and only—murder mystery. *Blood on the Dining-Room Floor*, most critics agree, is not first-rate Stein, but it is typical of her in one respect: It is truly mysterious. Although it contains the ingredients of a conventional detective story—a dead body, an array of suspects, a thick sprinkling of clues, an air of menace—it does not contain a solution. Who done it? Nobody knows.

A few years before she published *The Autobiography of Alice B. Toklas*, Stein had written the libretto (text) of an opera, *Four Saints in Three Acts*. Its music was composed by Virgil Thomson, a gifted young American Stein had met in 1925. Thomson, who had read and admired *Tender Buttons* when he was a student at Harvard, won Stein's heart when he set one of her early poems, "Susie Asado," to music. The two had become good friends and often discussed the possibility of collaborating on a long theatrical piece. Thomson proposed an opera based on the life of an artist; Stein wanted to base the work on George Washington. Finally, they scrapped both ideas and settled on the theme of saints.

Stein, who had always enjoyed reading about saints, was particularly interested in St. Teresa, whose birthplace she and Toklas had visited during their trip to Spain in 1912. Stein saw Theresa as a "real and practical" individual whose importance lay not in her actions but in her existence itself. "A

anybody else knows you are." Until now, she had written about the world just as she saw it, without thinking about how it might be received by readers. After the *Autobiography* became a best-seller, she was acutely conscious of her audience. "And how once you know the [book] buyer is there can you go on knowing that the buyer is not there?" she asked herself. In the winter of 1933–34 she behaved most uncharacteristically: She wrote nothing.

For Stein, not writing was almost like not breathing. She forced herself to

Paris itself—pictured is the Place de l'Opéra, in the heart of the city—was one of the stars of the Autobiography, *much of which takes place in the French capital.*

saint a real saint never does anything," she explained, "a martyr does something but a really good saint does nothing, and so I wanted to have Four Saints who did nothing and I wrote the Four Saints in Three Acts and they did nothing and that was everything."

The preamble, or opening section, of *Four Saints* includes a roll call of 21 saints, several lines to set the scene ("Imagine four benches separately," "A croquet scene and when they made their habits"), and the introduction of Teresa:

My country 'tis of thee sweet land of
  liberty of thee I sing.

Saint Therese something like that.
Saint Therese something like that.

The opera centered around Spanish saints, but Thomson's music reflected his own childhood in Missouri and the hymns of the Southern Baptist Church in which he had been raised. He set everything Stein had written, even the stage directions, to music, because he felt that every word was "part of the poetic continuity."

Talking about *Four Saints* later, Stein said it had been her intention to make the saints a "landscape." She explained that "a landscape does not move nothing really moves in a landscape but things are there, and I put into the play the things that were there." *Four Saints* ignores all theatrical conventions; it has no specific plot and no ordered sequence of events. Instead, as in much of Stein's work, all the events take place in what Stein called the "complete actual," or "continuous present."

Thomson and Stein completed their opera in early 1928, but their efforts to have it produced brought no results. At last, after *The Autobiography of Alice B. Toklas* had made Stein's name a household word, the Wadsworth Atheneum in Hartford, Connecticut, agreed to stage it. It would open in February 1934 as a kind of companion piece to the Picasso exhibition the museum had scheduled.

Thomson kept Stein informed by mail of his progress in getting *Four Saints* to the stage. He hired a designer for the costumes and scenery, a choreographer for the dance scenes, and a young playwright and future actor named John Houseman to direct the opera. Much impressed by performers he saw at a nightclub in New York City's Harlem, Thomson decided to engage an all-black cast for the opera. He also chose black performers because he felt that Stein's complex words would be understood by audiences only if the singers pronounced them clearly. White singers, said the composer, "just hate to move their lips," but black singers had "the most

perfect and beautiful diction." Although blacks had played black characters on Broadway, this was the first time that black singers and actors appeared in roles that could have been played by whites.

In December 1933, Thomson wrote to Stein to say that rehearsals had begun. "I have a chorus of 32 and six soloists, very, very fine ones indeed. [The] sets are of a beauty incredible, with trees made out of feathers and a sea-wall at Barcelona made out of

Ernest Hemingway prepares for an African hunting trip in the 1940s. Proud of his masculine image, he was enraged by Stein's depiction of him as "fragile" in the Autobiography.

95

Leo Stein, seen here with his wife, Nina (he married in 1921), was outraged by his sister's best-selling book. "Practically everything she says," he claimed, "is false."

Surrounded by elaborate, highly stylized scenery, the all-black cast of Four Saints in Three Acts plays a scene during the opera's hugely successful New York City run in 1934.

shells and for the procession a balda-chino [canopy] of black chiffon and bunches of black ostrich plumes just like a Spanish funeral. . . . The press is champing at the bit and the New York ladies already ordering dresses and engaging hotel rooms."

The press and the public were indeed eager to see the opera. Newspapers carried daily reports about the new show, and all tickets for the week-long Hartford run were sold out before the opening. After seeing a rehearsal, a major Broadway producer arranged to back the show in New York.

Opening night was a sensation. The bejeweled audience roared its ap-proval at the end, demanding one curtain call after another. One theatergoer, an elderly and dignifed historian, ripped off the collar of his ruffled evening shirt, punched in the top of his tall silk hat, and stood on his seat, shouting for the composer. All in all, as a friend reported to Stein, the evening was "a knockout and a wow."

The opera's run in New York City was equally spectacular. Tickets were sold for huge prices, and not a day passed that some news of the performance did not appear in the city's newspapers. Unaccustomed to seeing black performers in an opera, the critics outdid each other in praising the singers. One reviewer called the opera "inspired madness"; another said it was "the most important event of the season—important because it is theater and it flies off the ground, most important because it is delightful and joyous."

A few reviewers berated the play for its obscurity. "Pigeons on the grass, alas," said one, "is pigeon English." A popular columnist wrote, "I say it is spinach," and a leading music critic said that "a wine list would have made as good a libretto." Whether they loved it or hated it, however, New Yorkers vied for tickets and talked of little else.

Predictably, the spectacular success of *Four Saints* produced requests for its author's appearance. Stein's agent begged her to accept a lecture tour, but she refused. She had spoken in public on several occasions, and she had been struck with stage fright every time. "Don't you want to get rich?" asked her agent. "I do want to get rich," she replied, "but I never want to do what there is to do to get rich." Still, she was curious about seeing her native land after her long absence. She questioned friends who had returned from the United States: What did people eat? What were the new drugstores like?

Most of Stein's friends urged her to make the trip, but she continued to refuse. "It was really getting very exciting that we could not go," she wrote later, "it excited us and it was an

Stein works with composer Virgil Thomson on their opera, Four Saints in Three Acts. *The two later collaborated on* The Mother of Us All, *an opera about suffragist Susan B. Anthony.*

exciting thing to tell." At last, her curiosity and the pleas of her agent and her associates got the better of her. Late in the summer of 1934, she announced that she was about to write a series of lectures. She would deliver them, she said, in the United States. On October 17, she and Toklas boarded an ocean liner, the *Champlain*, at Le Havre, France, and set out for the land Stein had left 30 years before.

Returning to Europe from the United States in May 1935, Stein signs her autograph for a young admirer. She told reporters she had found everything in America "completely fascinating."

EIGHT

"Legends Never Die"

Yes I am married," said Gertrude Stein to a reporter in Paris. "I mean I am married to America, it is so beautiful." After spending more than six months in her native land, Stein was feeling almost like a foreigner in France, the country she had made her permanent home for more than 30 years. Her 1934–35 visit to the United States, she told the reporter, had made her feel "like a bachelor who goes along fine for 25 years and then decides to get married. That is the way I feel, I mean about America."

The American tour had been hectic, exciting, and triumphant. Stein had been awed by the size and scope of her homeland and by the warm welcome of its people. "I found that Americans really want to make you happy," she told an interviewer. "The fact that their gentleness has persisted while they have been becoming sophisticated shows that it is genuine."

America, in turn, had been delighted with its legendary daughter. "Put away any notion that Gertrude Stein is either slightly cracked, or a literary sideshow fakir of the kind [circus producer P. T.] Barnum liked to handle," read one of the many newspaper accounts of her cross-country tour. "This pleasing, thick woman with the close-cropped, iron-gray hair, the masculine face, and the marvelously pleasant smile, voice, and manner, is doing something.... good."

Stein followed up her trip to the United States with a book, *The Geographical History of America, or The Relation of Human Nature to the Human Mind*, published in 1936. Some of her admirers responded to it with enthusiasm; author Thornton Wilder said, "What a book! I mean what a book!... It's all absorbing and fascinating and intoxicatingly gay, even when it's terribly in earnest." Most readers,

German troops enter Paris in 1940. Stein had been shocked by the fall of France. "I had been so sure there was not going to be a war," she wrote, "and here it was, it was war."

Stein chats with a village family near her country home during World War II. Toklas and Stein's neighbors, who loved and respected the aging women, shielded them from the Nazis during the conflict.

however, found *The Geographical History* heavy and confusing; its sales were disappointing.

Stein's next book, *Everybody's Autobiography*, was more like the best-selling *Autobiography of Alice B. Toklas*. This time, however, instead of writing in the style in which Toklas spoke, Stein, as one critic put it, "followed her own conversational manner—discursive, chatty, warm, and often long-winded."

Many of today's literary scholars consider *Everybody's Autobiography* one of Stein's finest works; it speaks, writes Stein biographer Janet Hobhouse, "with the true and original voice of Gertrude Stein, without apparent art or bravado." Published in 1937, it was received with more critical praise than its predecessor, but its sales, too, were modest.

By 1937, Stein, along with other well-informed Americans and Europeans, was aware that international trouble was brewing once again. The fragile peace that had followed World War I was threatened by the civil war that was raging in Spain and, even more ominously, by the rise of fascist (highly nationalistic, frequently racist, and rigidly centralized) dictatorships in Germany and Italy.

Never at ease with her own father,

Stein had always equated world leaders with fathers, and fathers with trouble. "There is too much fathering going on just now," she wrote in *Everybody's Autobiography*. "Everybody now-a-days is a father," she continued. "There is father Mussolini [Italy's dictator] and father Hitler [Germany's Nazi leader] and father Roosevelt [the U.S. president] and father Stalin [dictator of the Soviet Union] and father Franco [leader of Spain's antidemocratic revolution]. . . . Fathers are depressing. . . . The periods of the world's history that have always been such dismal ones are the ones where fathers were looming and filling up everything."

Despite her forebodings, Stein did not think another major war was likely. However, as she wrote to a friend in April 1939, she realized that "accidents can happen and chips on shoulders can be knocked off." Chips would indeed be knocked off of many shoulders. After a three-year civil war, fascist leader Francisco Franco had defeated Spain's republican government in March 1939. On September 1, Germany invaded Poland; two days later, Britain and France declared war on Germany. By 1941, when Japan bombed the American naval base at Pearl Harbor, Hawaii, almost every country on the globe would be embroiled in World War II.

In 1939, most people in France, including Stein and Toklas, believed the war would not last long. Nevertheless, when France entered the war, the two women decided to stay at their country home in the village of Bilignin until the situation became clearer. For the 65-year-old Stein, who had not spent winter in the country since she was a little girl, the early war years were filled with adventure. "I did enjoy it," she wrote later. "There was snow and moonlight and I had to saw wood."

As the war increased in scope and ferocity, the adventure became a frightening one. The German army entered Bilignin in 1940, prompting the American consul in nearby Lyons to urge Stein and Toklas to leave France at once. Because the United States had not yet entered the war, the Nazi invaders would not have considered them enemy aliens, but they were Jews, and Hitler's violently anti-Semitic regime posed a deadly threat to all

Heralding the end of World War II, Allied troops land at Normandy, France, on D-Day, June 6, 1944. When she and Toklas heard the news, Stein wrote, "We were singing glory hallelujah."

members of the Jewish faith. Jews from all over Europe, including France, were being rounded up and sent to concentration camps. By the war's end, 6 million Jews would be dead at the hands of Hitler's Nazis.

"They all said 'Leave,' " wrote Stein later, "and I said to Alice Toklas, 'Well, I don't know—it would be awfully uncomfortable and I am fussy about my food. Let's not leave.' " The danger of remaining in German-occupied France was very real, but for the rest of the war years, Stein maintained her odd combination of naïveté and courage.

The two aging women stayed on, washing their clothes with wood ashes when their soap ran out and searching the woods for branches to burn in their fireplace when their coal supply was exhausted. They mastered the local peasants' art of fishing with a baited umbrella, and they sold their possessions, including some of Stein's paintings, to pay for the limited food available. "We ate Cézanne," commented Stein later.

Stein and Toklas were protected from the Germans by the officials of their village, who never reported their existence to the occupying army. Buoyed by the affection of their neighbors, Stein and Toklas remained optimistic. "You just go on talking to yourself in wartime," Stein wrote. "You talk to yourself about caterpillars but you never talk to yourself about spiders or lizards, you talk to yourself about

Stein beams as village children celebrate the liberation of France in 1944. "Thanks to the land of my birth and the land of my adoption we are free," she said. "Long live liberty."

dogs and cats and rabbits but not about bats or mice or moths."

By 1943, the war had cut Stein and Toklas off from all communication with friends outside and even inside France. At this point, Stein began writing a diary, which would eventually be published under the title *Wars I Have Seen*. In it she chronicled the almost invisible day-to-day life she and Toklas lived under the German occupation and recorded the larger events of the war as news filtered into Bilignin.

In January 1944, she wrote, "Nobody seems to think the war will ever end. We were all hopeful in '43, but in '44. . . . we have so much less hope of it ever being over so very much less hope." Her tone changed completely the following June, when the Allied armies at last invaded France. "Today is the landing and we heard [General Dwight] Eisenhower tell us he was here," she wrote with delight. "We were singing glory hallelujah, and feeling very nicely, and everybody has been telephoning to us congratulatory messages upon my birthday which it isn't but we know what they mean. And I said in return I hoped their hair was curling nicely, and we all hope it is, and today is the day."

Paris was liberated in August 1944, and in December Stein and Toklas returned to their beloved city. After five years in the country, the two were overjoyed to be back. "Landscape is all very well," observed Stein, "but you do long to see a street and streets." They grieved over the many friends whose wartime deaths they discovered and happily embraced those who had survived; among them was Stein's old friend Pablo Picasso. "I began to think the whole thing [had been] a nightmare," wrote Stein.

She was delighted to see the American soldiers who soon crowded Paris. She was, wrote her friend Virgil Thomson, "in love with GIs. Every day, as she walked her dog, she picked up dozens, asked them questions, took them home, fed them cake and whiskey, observed their language." Stein's sentiments were heartily returned by the young soldiers, who called her "Gertie." Her "love affair" with the American army would result in *Brew-sie and Willie*, a commentary on America written largely in soldiers' slang.

Wars I Have Seen was published in the spring of 1945 and greeted with an outpouring of critical and public praise. Stein's publisher, Bennett Cerf of Random House, sent her the first batch of complimentary reviews along with a note. "*Wars I Have Seen*," he said, "has been accorded a perfectly wonderful press and . . . the sale is already over the 10,000 mark. This will undoubtedly be by far the most popu-

Accompanied by her dog, Basket, Stein drinks tea with American soldiers in 1945. The sight of her countrymen delighted her. "Oh happy day," she wrote, "that is all that I can say oh happy day."

Toklas and Basket rest in front of the apartment they had shared with Stein. Virgil Thomson reported that after Stein's death, Toklas was "lonely in the large high rooms, but self-contained."

lar success you've ever had in America."

Stein continued to write, contributing articles to *Life* magazine, the *New York Times*, and the army newspaper *Yank*. At the request of American military authorities, she also visited army bases throughout Europe. Whether they had ever heard of Gertrude Stein or not, most of the men she talked to responded to this unusual, plain-spoken, energetic 71-year-old woman with warmth and affection. "Hiya, Gertie!" was their standard greeting.

Then, while visiting an army base in November 1945, Stein was suddenly stricken with severe abdominal pain. She recovered and continued her enthusiastic rounds, but the following July, a second attack brought her to a hospital outside Paris. Although her doctors suspected that she had cancer, they advised her not to have an operation until she had recovered some of her strength. Stein, by this time in great pain, was impatient. "I order you to operate," she told the surgeon.

On the afternoon of July 27, 1946, Stein awaited surgery with Toklas at her bedside. Somewhat dazed by sedatives, Stein looked at her friend and asked, "What is the answer?" Not trusting herself to speak, Toklas was silent. "In that case," said Stein, "what is the question?" They were her last words. Following surgery, which confirmed the diagnosis of cancer, she lapsed into a coma. At 6:30 that evening, Gertrude Stein was dead.

A giant had departed. The world mourned along with Alice B. Toklas, who would outlive her dear friend by 21 years. Newspapers and magazines carried long reports of Stein's death and almost reverent accounts of her life and work. An editorial in *The Nation* was typical. "Certainly she is not really dead," said the magazine. "Legends never die, and Miss Stein has made herself into an American legend.... Everybody in the world, from Picasso to a sergeant of the marines, came asking [her] for a sign and went away happy. . . . The world will be a duller place without her; her sins harmed no one; at this moment she is sitting in the Elysian fields talking to Samuel Johnson, the only man in the world who could ever be her match."

Within the year, the first of many books about Gertrude Stein began to appear. Her influence on both the literature and the art of her time was enormous. She was a shrewd and knowledgeable collector of paintings, and her support of such artists as Cézanne, Matisse, and Picasso helped launch the modern-art revolution. A literary pioneer, she explored forms and styles of writing uncharted by any author before her. Her resolute insistence on maintaining her own integrity and her own personal view of the world set her apart from the other writers of her time.

Stein's writing established no "school," or ongoing style, but it set a precedent for human expression. In the words of one of her most eminent biographers, John Malcolm Brinnin, "If there is going to be a continuing life of literature, it seems reasonable to assume that in the ghost that sings in the underworld of her 40 books—or in the flesh of someone who, like her, wants words to rise like Alhambras [castles] carved in air—she will come again."

Gertrude Stein cherished friendship, art, literature, conversation, and food. She also loved country music. Here, she sings her favorite song, "The Trail of the Lonesome Pine."

THE WORKS OF GERTRUDE STEIN: A SELECTED BIBLIOGRAPHY

BLOOD ON THE DINING ROOM FLOOR. Foreword by Donald Gallup. Pawlet, VT: Banyon Press, 1948.

BREWSIE AND WILLIE. New York: Random House, 1946.

EVERYBODY'S AUTOBIOGRAPHY. New York: Random House, 1937.

FERNHURST, Q.E.D., AND OTHER EARLY WRITINGS BY GERTRUDE STEIN. Edited with introduction by Leon Katz. Appendix by Donald Gallup. New York: Liveright, 1971.

THE GEOGRAPHICAL HISTORY OF AMERICA OR THE RELATION OF HUMAN NATURE TO THE HUMAN MIND. Introduction by Thornton Wilder. New York: Random House, 1936.

GEOGRAPHY AND PLAYS. Boston: Four Seas, 1922.

LECTURES IN AMERICA. New York: Random House, 1935.

LUCY CHURCH AMIABLY. New York: Something Else Press, 1969.

SELECTED WRITINGS OF GERTRUDE STEIN. Edited by Carl Van Vechten. New York: Random House, 1946. Includes *The Autobiography of Alice B. Toklas*, excerpts from *The Making of Americans*, portraits of Cézanne, Matisse, Picasso, "Melanctha," *Tender Buttons*, "Composition As Explanation," *Portrait of Mabel Dodge at the Villa Curonia*, "Susie Asado," "Preciosilla," "Ladies Voices," "Miss Furr and Miss Skeene," *Four Saints in Three Acts*, "The Winner Loses: A Picture of Occupied France," and an excerpt from *Wars I Have Seen*.

THREE LIVES. Norfolk, CT: New Directions, 1933.

FURTHER READING

Beach, Sylvia. *Shakespeare and Company.* New York: Harcourt, Brace, 1939.

Bloom, Harold, ed. *Gertrude Stein.* New York: Chelsea House Publishers, 1986.

Brinnin, John Malcolm. *The Third Rose: Gertrude Stein and Her World.* Boston: Little, Brown Books in Association with Atlantic Monthly Press, 1959.

Hobhouse, Janet. *Everybody Who Was Anybody: A Biography of Gertrude Stein.* New York: Putnam, 1975.

Hoffman, Michael J. *Gertrude Stein.* Boston: Twayne, 1976.

Mellow, James R. *Charmed Circle: Gertrude Stein & Co.* New York: Praeger, 1974.

Sprigge, Elizabeth. *Gertrude Stein: Her Life and Work.* New York: Harper Bros., 1957.

Sutherland, Donald. *Gertrude Stein: A Biography of Her Work.* New Haven: Yale University Press, 1951.

Toklas, Alice B. *Staying on Alone, The Letters of Alice B. Toklas, 1946–1967.* Edited by Edward Burns. New York: Liveright Publishers Corp., 1973.

CHRONOLOGY

Feb. 3, 1874	Born in Allegheny, Pennsylvania
1875	Moves with family to Vienna, Austria
1879	Returns to the United States
1893	Enrolls at Harvard Annex (later Radcliffe College)
1897	Enters Johns Hopkins University School of Medicine
1901	Leaves medical school without a degree
1903	Moves in with brother Leo at 27 rue de Fleurus, Paris
1905–1906	Poses for portrait by Pablo Picasso
1907	Meets Alice B. Toklas
1910	Publishes *Three Lives*, her first book
1912	Publishes "Portrait of Mabel Dodge at the Villa Curonia"
1914	Publishes *Tender Buttons*
1917	Works for American Fund for French Wounded during World War I
1922	Meets Ernest Hemingway/Publishes *Geography and Plays*
1925	Publishes *The Making of Americans*
1927–1928	Writes *Four Saints in Three Acts* with Virgil Thomson (produced in 1934)
1933	Publishes *The Autobiography of Alice B. Toklas*
1934–1935	Visits the United States with Toklas for lecture tour
1937	Publishes *Everybody's Autobiography*
1945	Publishes *Wars I Have Seen*
July 27, 1946	Dies in Paris

INDEX

PICTURE CREDITS

AP/Wide World Photos: pp. 76, 88, 98, 102;   Art Resource/Metropolitan Museum of Art: p. 58;   Art Resource/New York ADHGP: p. 82(left);   Art Resource/New York Spadem: pp. 55(left & right), 56, 57; Beinecke Library/Yale University: pp. 2, 16, 18(left), 20, 22, 24, 25, 30, 32, 36, 38, 39, 40–41, 42, 45, 46, 52, 54, 66, 74, 78, 79, 91, 96(left & right), 97, 103, 104;   The Bettmann Archive: pp. 12, 15, 27, 35, 49, 62, 67(right), 70, 77, 80(right), 81, 83, 84, 90, 94, 100(left), 101;   Cambridge Historical Society: pp. 34, 37;   Cone Archives/Baltimore Museum of Art: pp. 44, 53(bottom), 60, 64, 92;   Hemingway Collection: Kennedy Library: p. 81(left);   Courtesy of "i Taffi": p. 48;   New York Public Library: pp. 14, 40, 65, 100(right);   Oakland Public Library: p. 28; Philadelphia Museum of Art: p. 73;   Photoworld: p. 23;   N. Armstrong Roberts: p. 29;   Smithsonian Institution, Archives of American Art: pp. 50, 53(top), 71, 72, 73(left);   Springer/Bettmann Film Archive: pp. 17, 95;   UPI/Bettmann Newsphotos: pp. 18(right), 59, 63, 67(left), 69, 80(left), 85, 86, 93

Ann La Farge, a graduate of Radcliffe College and Columbia University, has taught in public and private schools and was an editor in New York City. She divides her time between Millbrook, New York, and New York City, where she lives with her four children.

Matina S. Horner is president of Radcliffe College and associate professor of psychology and social relations at Harvard University. She is best known for her studies of women's motivation, achievement, and personality development. Dr. Horner serves on several national boards and advisory councils, including those of the National Science Foundation, Time Inc., and the Women's Research and Education Institute. She earned her B.A. from Bryn Mawr College and Ph.D. from the University of Michigan, and holds honorary degrees from many colleges and universities, including Mount Holyoke, Smith, Tufts, and the University of Pennsylvania.